BABE DIDRIKSON ZAHARIAS

The Making of a Champion

BABE DIDRIKSON ZAHARIAS

The Making of a Champion

BY RUSSELL FREEDMAN

Clarion Books ☆ New York

CLARION BOOKS
a Houghton Mifflin Company imprint
215 Park Avenue South, New York, NY 10003

Copyright © 1999 by Russell Freedman

The text was set in 11-point Palatino.
Book design by Sylvia Frezzolini Severance.

Printed in the U.S.A.

Library of Congress Cataloging-in-Publication Data

Freedman, Russell.
Babe Didrikson Zaharias : the making of a champion / by Russell Freedman.
p.   cm.
Includes bibliographical references (p. 179) and index.
Summary: A biography of Babe Didrikson, who broke records in golf, track and field,
and other sports, at a time when there were few opportunities for female athletes.
ISBN 0-395-63367-2
1. Zaharias, Babe Didrikson, 1911–1956—Juvenile literature.
2. Athletes—United States—Biography—Juvenile literature.
3. Women athletes—United States—Biography—Juvenile literature.
[1. Zaharias, Babe Didrikson, 1911–1956. 2. Athletes. 3. Women—Biography.]
I. Title   II. Title: Making of a champion.
GV697.Z26F74   1999
796.352'092—dc21
[B]   98-50208
                                                            CIP
                                                            AC

CRW   10 9 8 7 6 5 4 3 2 1

☆ ☆ ☆

In memory of Dorothy Briley

☆ ☆ ★ ☆ ☆

Contents

Babe Didrikson jumps a hurdle.

☆ ☆ ☆ *One* ☆ ☆ ☆

BREAKING BARRIERS

As far back as she could remember, Babe Didrikson Zaharias lived only for sports, and she loved and excelled in them all. "Before I was even into my teens," she wrote in her autobiography, "I knew exactly what I wanted to be when I grew up. My goal was to be the greatest athlete that ever lived."

As a second grader, she won her school's marbles championship against girls and boys much older than she. From then on, she never looked back. She became an All-American basketball player, an Olympic gold medalist in track and field, and a championship golfer who won eighty-two amateur and professional tournaments. Along the way, she mastered tennis, played organized baseball, and was an outstanding diver, roller skater, and bowler. Her amazing versatility made her one of a kind. "Is there anything you don't play?" a reporter once asked. "Yeah, dolls," Babe replied.

For more than two decades, her wide, delighted smile appeared regularly in the nation's newspapers. Sportswriters called her "The Wonder

Girl," "The Super Athlete," or simply "The Babe," and the Associated Press poll of sports editors voted her Woman Athlete of the Year an unprecedented six times. In the eyes of many, she was and still is the greatest woman athlete of all time.

Babe was lavishly gifted, but she became a champion through relentless practice and a burning desire to excel. When she took up tennis, she played sixteen or seventeen practice sets a day. She ran the soles off a pair of tennis shoes every two weeks. "Oh, how that girl would *work* for the things she wanted," her sister Lillie recalled.

Proud of her skills, supremely self-confident, Babe loved the limelight and never hesitated to boast about her accomplishments. She tended to

Babe mastered tennis . . .

. . . and won eighty-two golf tournaments.

glamorize the story of her life, adding choice tidbits and details, putting a shine on past events. As impressive as her achievements were, she could not resist the temptation to embellish them. By the time she wrote her autobiography, the actual facts of her life were so entangled with the legend she created for herself that the line between them was often hazy. And yet her triumphs are entered in the record books for all to see. Babe

Didrikson Zaharias won more contests and broke more records than any woman in sports history.

She rose to fame in an era when women athletes had few chances for competition and were looked upon by many people as freaks or aberrations. "Girls in sports were [considered] tomboys and a little weird," according to Babe's friend and fellow golfer Peggy Kirk Bell. When Babe made headlines as an Olympic gold medal winner in 1932, the participation of female athletes in the Olympics was still a hotly debated, controversial issue. Baron Pierre de Coubertin, founder of the modern Olympic movement, had assailed women's sports as "against the laws of nature," an opinion shared by others who believed that competitive sports were too strenuous for "the weaker sex."

"You know, the ancient Greeks kept women out of their athletic games," said Avery Brundage, president of the Amateur Athletic Union. "They wouldn't even let them on the sidelines. I'm not so sure but they were right."

When Babe was growing up, those attitudes were being challenged. She was nine years old in 1920, when the nineteenth amendment to the Constitution finally gave American women the right to vote. That same year, the United States sent its first women's team—swimmers—to the Olympics. Women were demanding equality in many areas of life, and young women who loved sports had more opportunities than ever before.

Even so, competitive sports were still regarded as masculine territory. An aspiring female athlete had to confront society's strict view of what a proper woman should be and should do. Young Babe Didrikson seemed to defy conventional notions of femininity. She had the natural grace and buoyancy of a born athlete, but she was also tough, strong, ambitious, and fiercely competitive, with hacked-off hair and an unadorned face. Her battle to succeed as an athlete was, at the same time, a battle for the right to be herself, and her example helped break down barriers not just for women athletes, but for everyone. "Babe was a very brave girl or she could never have become the person she was," said her friend and former teacher Ruth Scurlock.

Golf was the game she loved most of all, and with her wisecracks, clowning, and trick shots, she brought a new sense of theater to the golf course. In 1947, she caused a sensation when she captured the British Women's Amateur golf championship, becoming the first American to win that historic tournament since its inception in 1893. "We have not seen a fairway phantom like her—not in 47 years," marveled a London newspaper. "What a Babe!"

Babe's first photo.

Two

THE WORST KID ON DOUCETTE

*H*er given name was Mildred Ella, but except for a few schoolteachers, hardly anyone addressed her as Mildred. Her family and friends, and later the world, knew her by her nickname, "Babe."

As an infant, the sixth of seven children of Norwegian immigrants, she was called "Baby." After her younger brother arrived, she became "Babe," a name adopted by the neighborhood boys when she began to hit home runs in sandlot baseball games. "Babe Ruth was a big [baseball] hero then," she recalled, "and the kids said, 'She's a regular Babe Ruth. We'll call her Babe.'"

Raymond Alford met Babe at one of those Saturday sandlot games in Beaumont, Texas. He became one of her best friends. "All the boys in the neighborhood would come and Babe was always there," he remembered years later. "Let me tell you, she was the only girl, but she was among the first to be chosen. She was not just hanging around to the last, no sir. . . . Ordinarily we didn't have anything to do with girls then. Babe was different. Once you saw her play, you didn't mind having her around."

Babe could never pass up a ball game. One day, her mother sent her to the grocery store to buy some hamburger for supper and told her to hurry. She ran all the way, bought the meat, and headed home. On the way back, she saw some kids playing baseball in the school yard. "I stopped to watch for a minute, and the next thing I knew I was in there playing myself," she wrote. "I laid the package of meat down on the ground. I was only going to play for a couple of minutes, but they stretched into an hour."

Finally she spotted her mother marching down the street, searching for her. "I got the meat, Momma," she yelled, moving out of the playground fast. "It's right here." She pointed to the spot where she had left the package. A big dog was standing there, lapping up the last of that hamburger.

"Poor Momma! She couldn't quite catch me," Babe recalled, "so she picked up an old piece of rope that was lying on the ground and swung it at me. She whipped me all the way home with that rope. I was running as fast as I could to stay ahead of her, but she could run fast too."

☆ ☆ ☆

Babe's father, Ole, liked to boast that his daughter had inherited her athletic ability from him. But Babe gave the credit to her mother, Hannah, who had been a champion skier and ice skater in her native Norway.

Hannah and Ole had married in Oslo, Norway. Ole Didriksen was a seafaring man, a ship's carpenter who had sailed around Cape Horn seventeen times. One of his voyages took him to Port Arthur, Texas, on the Gulf of Mexico, in the heart of America's booming oil-drilling industry. Port Arthur offered plenty of opportunities for an energetic young man, and when Ole sailed back to Norway, he told Hannah that the Gulf Coast would be a good place to settle down. In 1905, he returned to Port Arthur by himself and worked as a carpenter for three years before he saved enough money to bring his wife and three small children to America.

Hannah arrived in 1908 with the children—Ole, Jr.; Dora; and Esther Nancy. Four more children were born in Port Arthur: the twins Lillie and Louis in 1909; Mildred Ella, the future "Babe," on June 26, 1911; and Arthur, or "Bubba," in 1915.

While Babe was growing up, her family name was entered incorrectly in her elementary school records. Instead of "Didriksen," it was spelled

Ole Didriksen, Sr., with five of his seven children. Babe stands in front between the twins, Lillie and Louis. Ole, Sr., holds the baby, Arthur, in his arms, while Ole, Jr., sits on the porch beside his father.

"Didrikson." She never corrected the error and later adopted the changed spelling. Family members felt that she "liked the mistake," that "it was just another trait of Babe to be or do something that was different."

To accommodate his large family, Ole Didriksen built a house in Port Arthur that resembled a ship. But they didn't live there for long. Shortly after Bubba was born in the summer of 1915, a savage hurricane struck the Gulf Coast, uprooting trees and toppling church spires. Huge tidal waves surged through the streets of Port Arthur, flooding the Didriksens' sturdy, shipshape house. Rather than rebuild, Ole decided to move his family seventeen miles up the road to the thriving oil-refining center and shipping port of Beaumont. Babe had just turned four when Beaumont became their new home.

Ole bought a two-bedroom house at 850 Doucette Street in a gritty working-class neighborhood called the South End. The house wasn't nearly big enough for a family of seven kids, and as the years passed, Ole kept adding on to it until it became the biggest house on the block.

Doucette was a busy street with a trolley line running down the center. At one end of Doucette stood the sprawling Magnolia Oil Refinery, spouting steam and smelly gases from its many pipes and chimneys. At the other end of the long street were railroad tracks, over which oil-filled tanker cars constantly rolled north.

Babe grew up with a crowd of barefoot neighborhood kids who made Beaumont's South End their rough-and-tumble playground. They hitched rides on the backs of trolley cars and played baseball with mitts they got free by sending in Octagon laundry-soap wrappers. And they swam in the Neches River, braving its water moccasins and treacherous currents.

A short, wiry girl, Babe quickly became known as the local tomboy. She was a daredevil, always challenging the other kids to follow her on some reckless exploit. She would hang out at the railroad tracks with her sister Lillie, her closest childhood companion. They would hop on a moving freight car, wait until it was moving "faster 'n' faster 'n' *faster*," as Lillie recalled, and then jump off. "Sometimes we got skinned up," said Lillie, "but we never got hurt no worse than that."

A favorite Halloween stunt among the neighborhood kids was to rub soap on the Doucette Street trolley tracks, so the streetcar would slide and the motorman would have to slow down or stop. Then the ringleader—Babe, more often than not—would jump onto the back of the car and pull the trolley pole down off its wire, so the motorman would have to get out and replace it. Once Babe tripped and fell while she was running alongside the streetcar. She was nearly crushed under the car's wheels.

Growing up, she almost seemed to court trouble. At Magnolia Elementary School, her antics often sent her to the office of the principal, Effie Piland. "One day I heard the kids outside yelling for me," Mrs. Piland recalled. "I went outside and there was Mildred, sitting on top of the flagpole. She had climbed to the top and I told her to come down."

Students at Magnolia Elementary School in Beaumont, Texas. Babe is in the front row on the far left.

According to her brother Ole, Jr., Babe's stunts earned her a second nickname: "The Worst Kid on Doucette." Whenever a window was broken by a baseball, she was the one who got the blame. "She was just too active to settle down," Ole remembered. "She always wanted to be running, jumping, or throwing something."

Everyone who knew Babe recognized her passion for sports and her fierce determination to win any game she played. She could run faster, throw a ball farther, and hit more home runs than anyone her age, and she took pride in beating the boys at their own game. "She was the best at *everything* we did," said Lillie.

Babe and Lillie would often race each other down the block, except that Lillie sprinted along the sidewalk while Babe hurdled the hedges that separated the front yards along their street. There were seven hedges between the Didriksen house and the corner, but one was higher than the others, and Babe couldn't get over it. She went to the people who lived in that house and asked if they would mind cutting their hedge down to the right size. They agreed.

"I'd go flying over those hedges, and Lillie would race alongside me on the pavement," Babe wrote. "She was a fast runner, and had an advantage anyway, because I had to do all that jumping. I worked and worked, and finally got to where I could almost catch her, and sometimes beat her."

Like most of their South End neighbors, Babe's parents had to work hard to feed and clothe their family. "There were times when things were plenty tough," Babe recalled. "The toughest period . . . came when I was still a little kid. For several years there Poppa couldn't get work regularly. He had to go back to sea now and again when he couldn't find any jobs in Beaumont. And Momma took in washing."

The children had to help out, and all of them found after-school jobs just as soon as they were old enough. Babe mowed the neighbors' lawns and ran errands for the grocery store down the block. When she was in the seventh grade, she took a part-time job at a fig-packing plant. She had to peel the bad spots off the figs as they came her way, wash the figs in an acid solution, then toss them back into the trough. Later she worked at a potato-gunnysack factory, sewing up burlap bags for a penny apiece. She was fast, sewing a sack a minute, and was able to make very good money for a schoolgirl. "I'd keep a nickel or a dime for myself out of what I made," she wrote, "and put the rest in Momma's sugar bowl."

With such a large family, there were plenty of chores to be done at home, too. A big enclosed porch was wrapped around two sides of the house. It had sixteen windows that had to be washed and a floor that needed scrubbing. That was Babe's job. Her mother insisted that there was only one way to scrub a floor—on your hands and knees. But Babe had her own secret method. When her mother wasn't watching, she'd tie the scrub brushes to her feet and "skate" the floor clean, "whistlin' around like some ballet dancer on ice skates," Lillie recalled.

While times were often hard, the Didriksens had "a wonderful family life," as Babe remembered. There was always music in the house. Two of Babe's sisters played the piano, while her other sister played the violin. Her father played the violin, too. Her brothers played the drums. Her mother sang. And Babe played a thirty-five-cent harmonica she had

Babe (left) and Lillie with Arthur.

bought with money she saved by mowing lawns. "We had a family orchestra going there on the front porch at night after dinner," she wrote. "Other kids would gather around in our front yard. And you could see the lights going off in houses all up and down the block as people got through with their dishes, and came out on their own porches to listen."

Babe's father was a talented storyteller. He loved to spin fabulous yarns about his days at sea, holding his children spellbound with tales about storms and shipwrecks and desert islands. "What a bang we used to get out of his stories," Babe remembered. "We'd huddle around him and listen like mad. I'm not sure to this day whether he was kidding some of the time or not. . . . It could all be true. Things like that happened to those old seafarers."

True or not, Babe learned the art of storytelling at her father's knee, and when she became a famous athlete, she did not hesitate to embellish her own accomplishments in order to impress her listeners.

Ole Didriksen set up a gymnasium for his children under a big tree in the back yard. He made a weightlifting device out of an old broomstick with a flatiron at each end. And he put up bars for jumping and chinning, and a trapeze for acrobatic stunts. Babe and Lillie pretended that they were in the circus. A neighbor who lived across the street, whom they called Aunt Minnie, had been a real circus performer. She would come over and

Babe's parents, Hannah and Ole, around the time Babe entered high school.

show the girls how she could hang by her teeth and spin around. "When the circus came to town Aunt Minnie would take the whole bunch of us and show us everything," Babe recalled. "Then we'd come back home and try to do the acrobatics ourselves. Anything athletic I always seemed to enjoy."

Looking back years later, Babe admitted that she had not been an easy child to raise. "Poor Momma!" she exclaimed in her autobiography. Once, Hannah made Babe a beautiful new dress. The first time Babe wore that dress to school, she ripped it at the playground and came home with it torn and dirty.

When Hannah saw the damage, she really blew up. She went after Babe, forgetting that she had sprained her ankle getting off the streetcar a couple of days earlier. When Babe saw her mother hobbling toward her on that swollen ankle, trying to grab her, she said, "Momma, don't run. I'll wait for you." Hannah came up to Babe, ready to spank her: "Then she looked at me and began to laugh. She said, 'I can't whip you.'"

"My parents were strictly sweet," Babe wrote, remembering the gentle blend of love and discipline that marked her upbringing. "Some families don't show their love for each other," she added. "Ours always did." As Babe entered her teens, a rambunctious youngster who was not always accepted or understood, she knew that she could count on her family's unconditional love and approval. And with the warm certainty of their support, she had the self-confidence to try anything.

*Basketball practice. Babe (left) was high scorer for the
Miss Royal Purples.*

☆ ☆ ☆ *Three* ☆ ☆ ☆

A TEXAS TOMBOY

"As far back as I can remember I played with boys rather than girls," Babe once told a reporter. "The girls did not play games that interested me. I preferred baseball, football, foot-racing, and jumping with the boys, to hop-scotch and jacks and dolls, which were about the only things girls did. . . . I guess the habit of playing with boys made me too rough for the girls' games. Anyway, I found them too tame."

Babe was no ordinary girl—everyone recognized that. At David Crockett Junior High, her classmates admired her athletic skills and laughed at her jokes, but some of them felt that she really was too rough. "We all liked Babe," Edwina Lockhart recalled. "She was so good humored. We were afraid of her, though. She would go around hitting us on the arms with her knuckles to make our muscles knot up into 'frogs.'"

If some of the girls were afraid of her, some of the boys could not resist teasing and testing her. "The boys in my room continually teased Mildred, thumped and hit her when going through the halls," said Lenora Blanch, Babe's homeroom teacher at Crockett. "But that girl had a way of getting even out on the grounds. She would step on their heels and kick them. They didn't make anything off Mildred."

The teacher who knew Babe best at Crockett was Ruby Gage, who was in charge of physical education and playground activities. "We had intramural games between homerooms and the homeroom with Mildred on its team had it made," she remembered. "These games were very fiery and competitive. . . . [Babe] could master any sport she wanted to. Marbles—anything—you name it and she could do it better than anybody else."

When Babe entered Beaumont High School, she went out for every sport in sight. She won a swimming match sponsored by the YWCA and, with her classmate Lois "Pee Wee" Blanchette, easily captured the doubles crown in tennis. She was a member of the girls' baseball, volleyball, and golf teams, excelling at and reveling in every sport she tried. Her physical education teacher and coach at Beaumont High, a young woman named Beatrice Lytle, gave Babe her first formal training in several sports. Years later, Lytle remembered Babe Didrikson as a superb natural athlete.

"I saw possibly twelve thousand young women over those years," she said. "I observed them closely and I trained a lot of them to be fine athletes. But there was never anyone in all those thousands who was anything like Babe. I never again saw the likes of her. Babe was blessed with a body that was perfect. I can still remember how her muscles *flowed* as she walked. She had a neuromuscular coordination that is very, very rare."

Despite her skills, Babe did not, at first, win a place on the girls' basketball team, the Miss Royal Purples. "They said I was too small," she wrote. "I couldn't accept the idea that I wasn't good enough for the basketball team. I was determined to show everybody."

She spent hours practicing—dribbling, pivoting, passing, shooting baskets—and she pestered the coach of the boys' team for advice. "He took the time to help me," she wrote, "because he could see I was interested. . . . I'd say, 'Coach Dimmitt, tell those women I can play basketball!'"

Babe was a born athlete, not a scholar. While she never flunked a course, she worked just hard enough to pass the minimum three courses required to stay eligible for the school's teams. "I took my studies seriously because I wanted to be a teacher," said her tennis partner, Pee Wee Blanchette. "But Babe, well, she never had ideas like that about herself.

The Beaumont High girls' volleyball team. Babe is in the front row, on the left. The woman in the dark dress is the coach, Beatrice Lytle.

A power hitter in baseball, Babe (front row, third from left) poses with her fellow team members.

She was sports, nothing but sports. Babe never had any choice but to be a great athlete."

Babe eventually played on every girls' team at Beaumont High. "She wanted to excel," said her friend Raymond Alford. "She wanted to show you up. . . . I think her motives were probably a lot like mine. I knew that winning in sports was the only way I'd ever be recognized. Babe and I were both from poor families. If you did not have a car or if you did not have money, you were unacceptable. . . . Sports was a way of getting to be equal, and I think that's what carried Babe through and made her work so hard. . . . There was no other way to get ahead except sports."

Babe's single-minded devotion to sports set her apart from most of the other girls. "There was an academic group and an athletic group among the girls," recalled Ruth Scurlock, her English teacher. "Babe and her few friends in the athletic group wore denim skirts with pockets, socks like gym hose and flat oxford shoes. The others, the so-called society girls, wore their hair permanent waved. They wore silk stockings and high heels. These were the 'sissy girls' to Babe . . . but they were in the over-whelming majority and they were the leaders. It was terribly difficult for Babe to do what she wanted to do. Even in her own tough neighborhood, the other girls didn't like her because she was an athlete. Her very excellence at sports made her unacceptable to the other girls. She was an alien in her own land, believe me."

The most popular girls at Beaumont High belonged to a small, select group called the Kacklers Klub, which was dedicated to the support of Beaumont's male athletes. The Kacklers' motto was "Athletes are our favorite boys." And the chief requirement for membership was good looks and a pleasing personality. Babe was never invited to belong to the Kacklers, and she never expected to be. She was more interested in being cheered than in cheering others. Besides, she never wore jewelry, hated makeup, and didn't care about "fussy clothing."

"Babe was bucking society even then," said Ruth Scurlock. "She was simply being herself. She really had no other choice, I suppose."

But if Babe felt like an outsider—snubbed by the fashionable "society girls" and teased by some of the boys—she acted as though she couldn't care less. "She was just sure of herself," said one classmate. "She could do

In high school,
Babe favored denim skirts.

everything in athletics well, and she wasn't bashful about telling you about it."

She certainly wasn't bashful about standing up for herself. Once, she was challenged to a boxing match by "Red" Reynolds, the star halfback on the Royal Purple football team. "Go ahead, hit me as hard as you can," Reynolds taunted, sticking out his chin. "You can't hurt me!"

Babe *(right) with two members of the girls' swimming team.*

Babe took him at his word. She swung once, and Red dropped to the floor, senseless. "They were pouring water on me to clear the bells and birdies out of my head," he remembered. "That gal really gave me a K.O." For the rest of his life, Reynolds bragged about how he had been knocked out by the famous Babe Didrikson.

Babe loved pranks and practical jokes. Her cooking teacher remembered the time a big rat ran into the classroom. While everyone else "fled shrieking to high places," Babe herded the rat into a corner with a broom and claimed that she had captured it in a box. "She finally announced that the beast was gone, then as soon as everyone was back on the floor she maneuvered the rat out of a corner where she had [it] corralled and started the panic all over again." Babe thought that her joke was hilarious.

She could be boisterous and rowdy at times—"the rough and tumble type," as a classmate put it. "You couldn't win an argument with Babe," another schoolmate recalled. "She'd sure tell you off." But she was also a funny and entertaining girl, outgoing and down-to-earth, with a steadfast sense of loyalty to those who became her friends. "The same young woman that threw punches also warmed hearts," wrote her biographer, Susan E. Cayleff.

One of Babe's best friends at Beaumont High was her fellow athlete and teammate Bea Smith. "I liked her very much," Bea remembered. "She was friendly, and she was confident and fun-loving. Babe was just unique. She was kind of cocky, it's true, but I guess she had every reason to be, because as far as sports went, she was outstanding."

Babe finally made the varsity basketball squad in her junior year. She played forward, and from her first game, she was the team's high scorer, fast and aggressive on the court. "We were a terrific team," remembered

Babe (front row, second from left) with the Miss Royal Purples basketball team.

Pee Wee Blanchette. "The boys wouldn't admit it, but they liked the girls' team to play the same nights as they did because we brought such big crowds. The Miss Royal Purples didn't know what losing was, we never believed we'd ever lose. And we never did."

As the Miss Royal Purples traveled around the state, playing high school teams in other cities, sportswriters began to take notice of Babe. Texas newspapers ran headlines like BEAUMONT GIRL STARS IN BASKETBALL GAME and BEAUMONT GIRL STARS AGAIN. As a junior, Babe was named to both the all-city and all-state basketball squads.

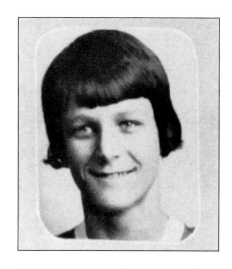

Babe's entry in the 1929 Pine Burr, *her high school yearbook.*

MILDRED "BABE" DIDRIKSEN

Forward

"Babe," has been a very necessary player on the Miss Royal Purple squad this year. She never failed to star in any game, at home or abroad. She is a very capable forward, who very seldom misses the basket. When "Babe" gets the ball, the scorekeeper gets his adding machine, and then he sometimes loses count. B. H. S. will have her again next year.

Early in 1930, Babe's team traveled to Houston, Texas, to play the girls from Houston Heights High. Watching from the stands that rainy February evening was Colonel Melvin Jackson McCombs, manager of the women's athletic program at a big insurance company. McCombs was scouting for new players. And he could not take his eyes off Babe Didrikson as the cocky, confident teenager scored twenty-six points, leading the Miss Royal Purples to victory and a state championship.

The Golden Cyclones in action. Babe, wearing Number 7 and plaid shorts, stands second from left.

☆ ☆ ☆ *Four* ☆ ☆ ☆

STAR OF THE GOLDEN CYCLONES

*M*elvin McCombs was always on the lookout for promising young female athletes. He was in charge of women's sports at Employers Casualty, a Dallas, Texas, insurance firm. Because he had been in the army once, everyone called him "Colonel."

Women's basketball was a popular spectator sport at the time, especially in the South and Midwest. Dozens of teams sponsored by corporations, churches, and clubs drew enthusiastic crowds as they competed in local and regional tournaments. Companies like Employers Casualty wanted to field winning teams, and they recruited the best players they could find.

McCombs had heard about Babe Didrikson's triumphs as the high-scoring star of the Miss Royal Purples, and he had traveled to Houston to see her in action. After the game, as Babe remembered, he introduced himself. "How would you like to play on a real big-time basketball team?" he asked.

"Boy, would I!" Babe replied. "Where?"

"At the Employers Casualty Company in Dallas. We're getting ready to go into the nationals in March."

McCombs told Babe that he could offer her a clerical job with Employers Casualty and a spot on the Golden Cyclones, the company's championship basketball team. She'd have a chance to play against some of the finest women's teams in the country. It was a wonderful opportunity for a sports-minded girl like Babe, but since she was a minor and still in school, she would have to get her parents' permission.

Babe's teammates were impressed, but she seemed to take McCombs's proposal in stride. "The rest of us were all excited," Thelma Hughes recalled. "But after the game, up in our rooms in the Rice Hotel, Babe didn't seem to be thinking about the offer. She was too busy leaning out the window trying to see how many people she could spit at and hit on the head when they walked below on the sidewalk."

Back home in Beaumont, Babe's parents held a family conference. Babe was eighteen and in her last year of high school. If she took a job with Employers Casualty, she would have to drop out of school before graduation and move to Dallas. Colonel McCombs had promised her $75 a month, a lot of money in that gloomy Depression year of 1930, when a skilled typist might make $50 a month. Babe would be able to help out her family.

Her father made the decision. That's why they had all come from Norway, Ole declared, to give the kids everything that America could offer. "You *go!*" he said, wagging his finger at Babe. And so she went to see her high-school principal, E. C. McDonald. According to Babe, she was allowed to withdraw from school, play out the season with Employers Casualty, then return to Beaumont to take her high-school graduation exams.

Three days later, Babe traveled with her father to Dallas, an overnight trip by train. "You never saw anybody more excited than I was that night at the railroad station in Beaumont," she wrote. "Here I was just a little old high-school girl, wanting to be a big athlete. And now I was getting a chance."

Colonel McCombs met them at the Dallas station in his yellow Cadillac and drove them to the offices of Employers Casualty, where Babe met the young women who would be her teammates. "I'd never seen so many large girls—large feet, and large hands," she wrote. "They were really husky." Most of the women worked in McCombs's department—accident and cyclone insurance for farmers and ranchers. That's why the company's teams were called the Golden Cyclones.

Babe arrived in Dallas on the morning of February 18, 1930. That night she played her first game for the Golden Cyclones against the Sun Oil Company team, the defending national champions. The Oilers had heard about Babe and meant to put her in her place. "They started hitting me that night, and they kept it up the whole season," she wrote. "If one guard fouled out against me, they'd send in another one. But I broke away for my share of shots." The Golden Cyclones won that game 48–18, and Babe was high scorer with fourteen points.

From then on, she starred for the Golden Cyclones in game after game. She wore No. 7, the same number she'd worn in high school, made her uniform over to fit like a glove, and was almost always her team's high scorer. In an era when women's basketball was played under different rules and twenty points was a respectable total for an entire team, Babe often scored thirty or more points a game.

Her office duties, meanwhile, were not very demanding. She learned to type on the job, and she had plenty of time to practice basketball. Women's sports at Employers Casualty were designed to gain favorable publicity and goodwill, and the company did everything possible to promote winning teams. The Golden Cyclones enjoyed first-class equipment, sleek orange uniforms, and expert coaching. The players were some of the best in the country. Like Babe, they had been hired mainly for their athletic skills.

Babe rented a $5-a-month room in the Oak Cliff section of Dallas, a quiet, tree-lined neighborhood where her teammates also lived. They all ate at the home of Danny Williams, the Golden Cyclones' assistant coach. His wife did the cooking. "She was a good cook," wrote Babe. "We paid 15 cents for breakfast and 35 cents for dinner." Babe got along very well on her salary. She sent $45 a month home to her parents. After paying for her room and meals, she had $10 a month to call her own.

She had been playing with the Golden Cyclones for just three weeks when she wrote to Tiny Scurlock, sports editor of the *Beaumont Journal*

Learning to type on the job.

and husband of Ruth Scurlock, Babe's English teacher: "Dear 'Tiny'—Boy I am still knocking them cold. . . . We played the Western Union Tuesday night and beat them 62 to 9. . . . Well to be frank with you I am going to make All American cause I have got my mind set on that."

That winter, the Golden Cyclones made it to the national women's basketball championships in Wichita, Kansas, sponsored by the Amateur Athletic Union (AAU). The Cyclones swept through to the finals, then lost the championship to Sun Oil by a single point. True to her prediction, Babe was chosen an All-American forward.

"Have gotten a lot of write ups from all of the leading newspapers in the South," she wrote to Tiny Scurlock. "I have a whole lot of fans now." Some of those fans were recruiters from rival companies who wanted to lure Babe away from Employers Casualty. They offered higher pay and

The Employers Casualty basketball team, 1931 national AAU champions. The arrow points to Babe.

better benefits if she would play for their teams. But she had a good reason to stay with Employers Casualty. Colonel McCombs was organizing a women's track-and-field team, and the prospect of competing in a challenging new sport was so tempting, Babe didn't want to think about changing jobs.

After the AAU basketball tournament in Wichita, she went home and finished up at Beaumont High. Then she began training for her first track-and-field meet. Babe had never seen a track meet until Colonel McCombs took her out to Lakeside Park in Dallas one Saturday afternoon, so she could watch the runners, jumpers, throwers, and hurdlers. "Those hurdles reminded me of all the hedge-jumping I'd done back home," she wrote. "I liked the looks of that event better than almost anything else."

McCombs had Babe try the javelin, the baseball throw, the shot put, the high jump, and the broad jump (now called the long jump). He gave her some basic instruction. Then she began to train. She had to be the greatest, the best, in any sport she tried, and she was willing to work hard. "I trained and trained and trained," she wrote. "I've been that way in every sport I've taken up."

Members of the Golden Cyclones track-and-field team were given time off from the office to practice in the afternoon, but that wasn't enough to satisfy Babe. "I'd go out to Lakeside Park at night and practice by myself until it got dark, which wasn't until nine or nine-thirty at that time of year," she wrote. "If there was good clear moonlight, I might keep going even longer."

The night before her first track meet, she worked extra hard. She practiced her step timing for the broad jump and for the high jump. She spent about two hours at that, then finished off by running the 440-yard dash. Instead of pacing herself, she wanted to see if she could sprint all the way.

Flying over the hurdles.

"Well, I just barely made it to the finish line," she wrote. "I fell face down on the grass. I was seeing stars. I must have laid there fifteen or twenty minutes before I could get up."

When she told Colonel McCombs about it the next morning, he said, "What are you trying to do, kill yourself?"

"I think he admired me for working so hard," wrote Babe.

As Babe intended, the hard work paid off. In her first track meet, in May 1930 at Southern Methodist University, she entered four events—the broad jump, the high jump, the 100-yard dash, and the 440-yard dash. She won all of them.

That summer, in a succession of track meets, Babe seemed unbeatable. She took the first ten gold medals she won and made a bracelet out of them. By her nineteenth birthday on June 26, she had collected eighteen gold medals. And by the time the track season ended in September, she held southern AAU records in the high jump, the eight-pound shot put, and the broad jump, and national AAU records in the javelin and baseball throw. Her 1930 javelin throw of 133 feet 6 inches was unofficially considered a world record before 1932, when officials began to keep more formal records.

Bursting with confidence, Babe told Tiny Scurlock: "Oh! yeah! Right after the Track season I am gonna train for the Olympic[s] in 1932."

Babe also competed on the other Employers Casualty teams. She played doubles tennis, was a power hitter in softball, and performed in exhibitions of springboard and platform diving. The company's diving team was billed as "Mildred Didrikson and her Employers Casualty Girls." But it was in basketball and track and field that Babe really shone.

During the 1931 basketball season, she scored an average of thirty-two points per game as she led the Golden Cyclones to an AAU national championship. Once again, she was selected an All-American. That summer, she continued to collect gold medals in track-and-field events. At the national AAU meet in Jersey City, New Jersey, she had the admiring eye of the entire sports press as she set new records in the baseball throw, broad jump, and 80-meter hurdles. Sports columnist Arthur Daley of the *New York Times* called her "A new feminine athletic marvel . . . this remarkably versatile girl" and reported that the "crowd of 15,000 looked on in amazement" as Babe went through her paces.

An outstanding swimmer and diver.

Babe caused tremendous excitement that day in Jersey City. When the AAU meet ended, the crowd poured out of the stands onto the field to get a closer look at this phenomenal new star. Mounted police had to move in to clear the field. Back in Texas, the *Dallas Morning News* ran a big photo spread of Babe, calling her the "ace of the local Golden Cyclones" and "the world's outstanding all round feminine athlete."

Two years earlier she had been playing sandlot baseball. Now she was garnering headlines as the world's best. Babe was enormously proud of the press coverage she was getting. "My picture was in the center, blown way up big," she boasted of one newspaper story. "There were just little head shots of the others. Man, I just loved that!"

She had never been shy, and she had plenty to brag about now. Her cocky attitude offended some of her teammates, who complained that she was no longer the "modest, likeable girl" they had once known. "I admit I admired Babe because of all the things she could do," one teammate recalled, "but some of the other gals really resented her. . . . she was out for Babe, honey, just Babe."

(RIGHT) *Babe wins the running broad jump with a leap of 17 feet 11½ inches at the women's national AAU track-and-field meet in Jersey City, New Jersey, July 1931.*

(BELOW) *Babe sets a new record in the 80-meter hurdles at Jersey City.*

Babe felt that her teammates were envious. What they really resented, she suspected, was all the attention she was getting. But she worried about their chilly attitude and considered leaving the Cyclones for another team. "Heck, 'Tiny,'" she wrote, "if I get me another [offer], I'm gonna take it. . . . These girls are just like they were in Beaumont High School. Jealous and more so because they are all here and trying to beat me. But they can't do it."

Babe reacted by becoming even more boastful and cocky than before. She cultivated a swaggering, hard-boiled, tough-kid image, wore her hair in a short bob, and dressed as she pleased. When a reporter commented on her "masculine" features and "almost complete absence of feminine frills," Babe told him, "I know I'm not pretty, but I do try to be graceful."

In the eyes of her teammates, she was a brash and self-centered young woman, and she was judged harshly. But her boasting, more than anything, was a display of the confidence she felt in her abilities and an expression of her joy in winning. An athlete needs that kind of confidence to be a winner. If Babe had been a young male athlete, her boastful posturing would have been considered healthy and natural. As a young woman during the early 1930s, however, she was expected to be modest and demure.

Portrait of Babe
around 1930.

Meanwhile, she was under constant pressure to send home as much money as she could. America's Great Depression, a bleak and discouraging period of widespread unemployment and poverty, had started with the stock market crash of 1929 and seemed to be getting worse all the time. Babe's father was having trouble finding work, and the family had come to depend heavily on Babe's help. She managed to get a raise from Employers Casualty to $90 a month, but her salary never seemed enough. And she received no bonuses or extra pay for her athletic triumphs. "Babe's family always had their hands out to her," said Ruth Scurlock. "She was under a lot of pressure all the time. She never had as much money as they thought she did, but they wanted her to give, give, give."

Despite these worries, 1932 turned out to be a banner year for Babe. She played brilliantly during the basketball season and was named an All-American for the third year in a row. Then she began to train in earnest for the AAU national track-and-field championships, to be held in Evanston, Illinois, in July. That year, the AAU meet and the Olympic tryouts were being combined in a single event. Those athletes who were successful at Evanston would also win places on America's 1932 Olympic team.

Babe had worked out a strenuous training program with Colonel McCombs, one designed to build her strength and endurance for the all-important AAU meet. Up at dawn, she would run two miles before breakfast, then shower and eat, then go out to the field to practice every event she wanted to enter. She was given plenty of time off to get herself ready.

One day at work, McCombs called Babe into his office. "I've been studying the records of the girls on the other teams that will be in the meet," he said. "I think if you enter enough different events . . . you can do something that's never been done before. I believe we can send you up there to represent the Employers Casualty Company and you can win the national championship for us all by yourself."

McCombs had great confidence in Babe, but he worried about her intensity, her almost fanatical determination to win. "Never before in my life have I seen a man or a woman to compare with Babe Didrikson for natural ability," he told a reporter. "She has no equal. Her only fault . . . is that she unconsciously and unknowingly overtrains. Also Babe's juvenility and nervous energy ofttimes work to her disadvantage. She has a tendency to brood over coming events."

Showing perfect form in the baseball throw.

☆ ☆ ☆ *Five* ☆ ☆ ☆

THE ONE-WOMAN TEAM

*T*he AAU women's track-and-field championships would be the biggest test that Babe Didrikson had ever faced. If she could win the national team championship for Employers Casualty, she would qualify for the 1932 Olympics, scheduled for Los Angeles later that year.

The combined AAU meet and Olympic trials were being held at Dyche Stadium in Evanston, Illinois, just north of Chicago. Babe traveled to Chicago by overnight train with Mrs. Henry Wood, the official chaperone or "team mother" of the Golden Cyclones, who had insisted that Babe buy a dressy outfit to wear during the trip.

A battery of reporters and photographers was waiting to meet them at Chicago's Union Station. Babe posed for pictures and radiated confidence, boasting that she would win every event she entered. "Miss Mildred Didrikson, the sensational young lady from Dallas, Texas, is expected to be the standout of the meet," reported the *New York Times*.

Usually Mrs. Wood had an entire team to look after, but that evening, at their Chicago hotel, she had enough worries with Babe alone. Babe may

In her hotel room, Babe admires the new hat and dress she bought especially for her trip to Chicago.

have seemed confident, but inside she was seething. She was so keyed up that she couldn't sleep. She tossed and turned in bed, then got up and paced about the room. In the middle of the night, she began to complain of stomach pains. When she placed her hand on her belly, "the hand would just bounce up and down," she wrote.

Mrs. Wood was alarmed. She feared that Babe might be having an appendicitis attack, and she finally called the hotel doctor. He came to the room, examined Babe, and found nothing wrong but a case of "nerves." It was nearly dawn before Babe and Mrs. Wood finally fell asleep.

A few hours later, Babe awoke in a panic. The sun was up. The day was already hot and humid. They had both overslept. There was barely enough time to get themselves ready and make it out to Evanston. They pulled on their clothes, hurried downstairs, and hailed a cab. During a frantic ride through heavy Chicago traffic, it became obvious that Babe would never have time to change at the stadium. As the taxi broke out of the traffic jam and raced toward Evanston, Babe climbed into her blue-and-white track suit in the back seat while Mrs. Wood held a blanket around her.

They pulled up in front of Dyche Stadium just as the opening ceremonies were about to begin. Babe jumped out of the cab and dashed into the big concrete arena. Inside, more than two hundred women athletes dressed in their team colors were milling about and waiting. As each team was announced over the loudspeaker, the women jogged out onto the field while several thousand sports fans filling the grandstand whistled and applauded. Some teams had fifteen members or more, and the biggest one, the Illinois Women's Athletic Club, had twenty-two.

When Babe's team was called, the loudspeaker announced: "MILDRED 'BABE' DIDRIKSON, REPRESENTING THE EMPLOYERS CASUALTY COMPANY OF DALLAS, TEXAS."

Babe ran onto the field grinning broadly and waving her arms wildly above her head. When the crowd saw that she was all alone, a solitary one-woman team, many people rose to their feet and cheered. "You never heard such a roar," she recalled. "It brought out goose bumps all over me."

Most of the athletes were entered in one or, at the most, two or three events. Because Babe was the sole member of her team, officials had stretched the rules and allowed her to enter eight of the ten events. Since she had to compete in both the qualifying and final rounds, she had to run from one event to another.

"For two-and-a-half hours I was flying all over the place," she wrote. "I'd run a heat in the eighty-meter hurdles, and then I'd take one of my high jumps. Then I'd go over to the broad jump and take a turn at that. Then they'd be calling for me to throw the javelin or put the eight-pound shot." The only events she did not enter that day were the 50-yard and 220-yard dashes. As soon as she finished one event, they were already calling her for the next.

On a few occasions, the judges delayed starting so that Babe could rest

(LEFT) *Winning the 80-meter hurdles in the Olympic tryouts at Evanston, Illinois, July 1932.*

(BELOW) *"The payoff on all that hedge-hopping," said Babe (far right).*

and catch her breath. Some of the other athletes complained that she was getting special treatment. It didn't help matters when she marched around the infield hollering, "I'm going to win everything I enter!"

Halfway through the meet, spectators in the stands began to realize that Babe Didrikson had a fighting chance to win the AAU team championship singlehandedly. Each time Babe took her place for another event, silence fell over the stadium. When she won, the crowd roared its approval. When she lost, the entire grandstand seemed to groan.

That afternoon the temperature climbed past 100 degrees. One of the athletes, Jean Shiley, remembered, "It was so hot that one of the girls ordered a 100-pound block of ice and we all took turns sitting on it." Despite the tension and heat, Babe seemed to sail through the afternoon, swept along by the cheers of the crowd. "It was one of those days in an athlete's life when you know you're just right," she recalled. "You feel you could fly. You're like a feather floating in air."

After her last event, she jogged off the field sweating and panting. Mrs. Wood was standing there, crying. "Babe!" she called through her tears. "You did it! You did it! You won the meet all by yourself!"

Babe had won first place in five events: 80-meter hurdles, javelin, shot put, baseball throw, and broad jump. She tied for first in the running jump. She placed fourth in the discus throw and failed to qualify in the 100-yard dash. All together, she scored thirty team points, winning the national championship for the Golden Cyclones. The second-place team, the Illinois Women's Athletic Club, scored twenty-two points.

Babe's performance on that sweltering afternoon was one for the books. In the space of three hours she collected six gold medals and broke four recognized women's world records. Three of them were records she herself had set during the past two seasons. She topped her old marks by hurling a baseball 272 feet 2 inches, throwing the javelin 139 feet 3 inches, and running her first heat in the hurdles in 11.9 seconds. Her fourth world record was the running high jump—5 feet 3 3/16 inches. But in that event, she had to share the new record with Jean Shiley, the athlete who tied her for first place. Although she had rarely performed in the shot put, she set an AAU and a U.S. record in that event with a toss of 39 feet 6 1/4 inches. And she won the broad jump with a leap of 17 feet 6 inches.

With Jean Shiley of Philadelphia, who tied Babe for first place and a new world record in the high jump at Evanston.

When the meet ended, Babe strolled around the field, waving to people, playing her harmonica, and chatting with the sports reporters and photographers who crowded around her. George Kirksey, who covered the meet for the United Press, described Didrikson's outing that afternoon as "the most amazing series of performances ever accomplished by any individual, male or female, in track and field history."

That evening, Babe and Mrs. Wood went out to celebrate with some friends. Babe loved to dance, and on this festive occasion, "we danced until three o'clock in the morning." The next day, Babe put herself through a good workout "to make sure that my muscles didn't tighten up." The Olympic Games in Los Angeles were next. "Gangway!" one newspaper warned. "Here comes a real woman athlete. With the speed and grace of an antelope."

Babe's newly chosen Olympic teammates were the first to acknowledge her impressive skills, but they did not appreciate an Associated Press story that appeared in newspapers across the country. "Miss Mildred Didrikson of Dallas, Texas, who prefers to be called 'Babe,' will lead the American women's Olympic track and field team," reported the AP. "Such assistance as she may need against the foreign invasion will be provided by fifteen other young ladies."

Babe stands on the winner's platform at the 1932 Olympics in Los Angeles after setting a new world record in the 80-meter women's hurdles. She is flanked by Evelyne Hall (left) of the United States, who came in second, and Marjorie Clark of South Africa, third.

☆ ☆ ☆ *Six* ☆ ☆ ☆

GOING FOR THE GOLD

*B*abe and her teammates left Chicago's Union Station on the morning of Monday, July 18, bound for California. They traveled in style, occupying their own Pullman car with a big red, white, and blue banner on its side that read U.S. OLYMPIC TEAM.

A cross-country train trip was regarded as a great adventure in the 1930s. Few of the women had ever traveled on a "sleeper," a special car with seats that convert into upper and lower berths at night. "We felt like millionaires," one of them recalled. "It was a dream."

During the five-day trip, Babe spent much of her time working out in the aisles, while, according to her, "most of the girls sat around watching the scenery and playing cards and gabbing. . . . Several times a day I'd jog the whole length of the train and back. People in the other cars took to calling out, 'Here she comes again!'"

Her antics embarrassed some of her teammates. "Babe was very full of herself and on the train she was always pulling pranks," recalled Evelyne Hall, who would compete against Didrikson in the 80-meter hurdles at

Los Angeles. "She delighted in yanking the pillows out from under your head when you were asleep. She . . . also used to take ice from the water cooler and drop it down our backs."

Babe's sense of fun didn't appeal to everyone. "She had no social graces whatsoever," said Jean Shiley, who had been elected team captain. "She constantly wanted to be on center stage. . . . It was impossible to get to know her because she was always chattering, talking, bragging. . . . She ran around with her medals from Evanston, saying, 'I'm the greatest, no one's better than me, Babe Didrikson.' Today, I don't think her behavior would seem so outrageous. People are used to flamboyant athletes. In those days, athletes were supposed to be full of humility and modesty."

When the special train pulled into the Union Pacific Station in Los Angeles on the morning of July 23, the athletes stepped down from their Pullman car in high spirits, singing "Hail, Hail, the Gang's All Here." Jean Shiley spoke for the team as she told reporters that they were "by no

The American women's track-and-field team arrives in Los Angeles to compete in the Olympic Games. Babe stands in the rear, third from the right.

means overconfident." They intended to train seriously and do their very best. Babe wasn't as modest. "I came out here to beat everybody in sight and that's just what I'm going to do," she announced. "Sure, I can do anything!"

If her teammates felt that Babe was loud and self-centered, sportswriters covering the Olympics saw her as a colorful personality with a healthy Texas ego and an engaging down-home frankness. "The Babe is no boaster and no braggart," said the *New York Times*. "She tells you simply what she can do, and then she does it."

Babe was good copy. She was always willing to talk, and she became a favorite of both the press and the public. Her optimism, her exuberant outbursts of confidence, struck a sympathetic chord with millions of worried Americans who were struggling to get by that year.

The 1932 Olympics took place in the depths of the worldwide economic depression. People looked to the pageantry of sports and the exploits of sports heroes for inspiration as well as for escape. Athletes were seen as larger-than-life figures who offered a vision of hope that hard work and persistence could be rewarded. They seemed to demonstrate that ordinary humans could win against heavy odds, and that the challenges of real life, too, could be conquered. Babe's humble working-class background was widely known, and she was admired as one of the outstanding athletes in the Olympic Games.

At the time, women were still something of a novelty as Olympic competitors. Track-and-field events for women had made their first appearance on an experimental basis at the 1928 Games, and as late as 1931, the International Olympic Committee had seriously considered eliminating all women's events. During the 1932 Games, male athletes were housed in the lavish new "Olympic Village," the first ever built, while the women were put up at the rather ordinary Chapman Park Hotel.

Babe and her teammates had arrived in Los Angeles a week before the opening of the Games. They used that time to train for the events they were going to enter, to meet with the press, and to mingle with the Hollywood stars who converged on the Olympic site. Screen idols were everywhere, rubbing shoulders with the athletes and posing for photographs with them. "I got to meet a number of Hollywood stars I'd seen on the screen,"

Rubbing shoulders with the athletes: (left to right) swimmer Helene Madison, sportswriter Grantland Rice, Babe Didrikson, humorist Will Rogers, swimmer Georgia Coleman, sportswriter Braven Dyer.

said Babe. "There was Clark Gable—he could really keep you laughing. And I spent some time with Will Rogers, too. He was another wonderful fellow."

Even in this glamorous crowd, Babe Didrikson stood out. Reporters who were drawn to her by her athletic feats were won over by her warmth and her unpredictable sense of humor. Even when she boasted, which was most of the time, her folksy, down-to-earth way of speaking had reporters quoting her endlessly. More than once, she had been praised for her superb "neuromuscular coordination." Sportswriter Grantland Rice had hailed her as "the most flawless section of muscle harmony, of complete mental and physical coordination the world of sport has ever known."

Babe translated this in her own way: "Folks say that I go about winning these athletic games because I have the cooperation thing that has to do with eye, mind, and muscle. That sure is a powerful lot of language to use about a girl from Texas, maybe they are right about it. All I know is that I can run and I can jump and I can toss things and when they fire a gun or tell me to get busy I just say to myself, 'Well, kid, here's where you've got to win another.' And I usually do."

Although Babe turned twenty-one a few days before the Games opened, she was widely believed to be nineteen. On her application form for the Olympics she had fudged a bit, writing in her penciled girlish scrawl that she was born in 1913, rather than 1911. And when reporters hailed her as a teenage athletic marvel, she did not bother to correct them.

☆　☆　☆

The Tenth Olympiad at Los Angeles extended from July 30 to August 14, 1932. Thirteen hundred athletes, one tenth of them women, took part in the spectacular opening ceremony before a capacity crowd of 105,000 at the Los Angeles Coliseum, while 50,000 more people swarmed about outside, hoping for a glimpse of the ceremony. It was up to then the biggest crowd ever to see an Olympics, and the first of the lavish opening ceremonies that would become an Olympic tradition.

A 250-piece band and a white-robed choir of 1,200 voices joined in a rousing rendition of "The Star-Spangled Banner." Then marching ranks of tanned and healthy athletes paraded into the stadium, beginning, as tradition dictated, with the delegation from Greece, and ending with the host Americans. The American women's team included swimmers, divers, and fencers as well as track-and-field athletes—thirty-seven women in all. They waited their turn in the main tunnel leading to the field, then emerged from the darkness into the blinding California sunlight for their first look at the immense crowd. They wore uniforms of white skirts and blouses, red vests and hats, and stiff new shoes.

After an artillery salute and the Olympic flag-raising, two thousand pigeons were released into the air. Trumpets blared, the Olympic flame was lit, and the assembled athletes, standing in columns that stretched across the field, repeated the words of the Olympic oath in a dozen different languages. Then they stood patiently under the hot sun while the vice-president of the United States and other dignitaries made welcoming speeches.

The opening ceremonies of the Tenth Olympiad at the Los Angeles Coliseum. Thirteen hundred athletes from around the world stand on the field as they watch the symbolic release of two thousand pigeons.

"To tell you the truth," Babe admitted later, "I couldn't enjoy the ceremonies that much after we got out there. We all had to wear special dresses and stockings and white shoes that the Olympic Committee had issued to us. I believe that was about the first time I'd ever worn a pair of stockings in my life. I was used to anklets and socks. And as for those shoes, they were really hurting my feet."

Babe felt that those shoes were getting tighter and tighter. She listened to the speeches, studied the shirt-sleeved crowd in the grandstands, and counted the flags of participating nations fluttering in the breeze around the stadium. But her feet were killing her. Finally she kicked off both shoes. The woman standing behind her noticed this and kicked off her shoes, too. By the time the speeches ended, practically every woman in the American contingent had her shoes off.

The next day, the competition began. Six track-and-field events were open to women that year. The Olympic Committee had ruled that a single athlete could compete in no more than three events. Babe entered the javelin throw, the 80-meter hurdles, and the running high jump, events in which she had set records two weeks earlier in Evanston.

The javelin throw was held late in the afternoon on the first day of competition. Each contestant was allowed three tries. Babe waited at the side of the field, swinging her arms and stretching nervously. When her

Warming up for the javelin throw.

turn came for her first throw, she paused briefly, left hand on her hip, holding the javelin about ear level over her shoulder. Rising slightly on her toes, she started down the runway, drew back her arm, rotated to the right, and with a hop-step, let the javelin fly. As she did, her hand slipped off the cord on the handle and she felt a sharp pain in her right shoulder.

Instead of soaring in a high arc as it usually did, the javelin zoomed along close to the ground "like a catcher's peg from home plate to second base," Babe recalled, before finally slicing into the ground. Babe had set an Olympic record and had broken her own recognized world record by more than four feet with a throw of 143 feet 4 inches. When the new record was announced over the loudspeaker, the stadium erupted with cheers and applause. Babe trotted about the field, her hands clasped high above her head.

Her face was beaming, but her shoulder hurt. Years later she revealed that she'd been unable to warm up properly because of the crowd on the field. "Nobody knew it, but I tore a cartilage in my right shoulder when my hand slipped making that throw," she wrote. "On my last two turns, people thought I wasn't trying because the throws weren't much good. But they didn't have to be." No other competitor came close to Babe's new record. She had won her first Olympic gold medal.

Two days later, the qualifying heats for the 80-meter hurdles were held. Again, Babe was hoping to break both the Olympic record and her own world record. She did both in the qualifying heat, completing the course in 11.8 seconds—a tenth of a second faster than the time she had set in Evanston.

The finals of the 80-meter hurdles were held the next day. Babe's chief rival was her teammate Evelyne Hall. As the runners knelt at the starting line, Didrikson and Hall were in lanes side by side. Babe was a bit too anxious. She jumped the gun, and everyone was called back. Jumping the gun twice meant automatic disqualification. The runners knelt again, and when the gun cracked, Babe held herself back for a split second, until she saw the other runners in front of her. Then she surged forward.

Evelyne Hall was ahead, leading by a stride over the first hurdles. Babe closed in on her with powerful leaps and then pulled even. The two athletes were neck and neck as they cleared the last two hurdles. They

Babe (right) on her way to a new world record of 11.8 seconds in the qualifying heat of the 80-meter hurdles.

appeared to be absolutely even when their feet touched the ground just before the finish line. As they hit the tape together, Babe threw up her arm and yelled to Hall, "Well, I won again!"

The official timer declared that both women had reached the tape in 11.7 seconds—a new world record. It looked like a dead heat. The judges huddled in confusion and took nearly half an hour to make their decision. Finally, they declared Babe Didrikson the winner. She was awarded her second gold medal.

An "eye-lash victory." Evelyne Hall (right) and Babe Didrikson breaking the tape in the finals of the 80-meter hurdles.

Sportswriter Arthur Daley of the *New York Times* called it an "eye-lash victory." Other reporters who were on the scene set Babe's margin of victory anywhere from two to six inches, but it remained a controversial decision and a bitter disappointment for Evelyne Hall. Photographs and film footage of the race, viewed later, did not show the winner beyond any doubt. "If it was horse racing," Babe said later, "you'd say I won by a nose." She added that her victory was "the payoff on all the hedge-hopping" she had done as a girl in Beaumont.

Babe's double Olympic victory—two gold medals in two events—made headlines all over the country. It now seemed possible that she could win a third track-and-field gold medal in a single Olympic year, something that no woman had done. Excitement mounted as she prepared for her third and final event, the running high jump.

Once again, her chief rival was a teammate, Jean Shiley, the captain of the American team and the athlete who had tied Didrikson for first place in the high jump at Evanston. On the day of the event, all other competitors had dropped out by the time the bar had been raised to 5 feet 5 inches—nearly two inches higher than the record that Didrikson and Shiley had set jointly in Evanston. Both women cleared that height, setting a new world record. To break the tie, a jump-off had to be held. The judges raised the crossbar an inch, to 5 feet 6 inches.

Jean Shiley was up first. She failed to clear the bar. Then it was Babe's turn to try for her third gold medal. Sportswriter Grantland Rice described what happened: "There was a wild shout as Miss Didrikson cleared the bar by at least four inches. It was the most astonishing jump any woman ever dreamed about. But luck was against her. As the Babe fluttered to earth her left foot struck the standard a glancing blow, just six inches from the ground—and the crossbar toppled into the dust with her."

The judges ruled that Babe's jump was a miss. They dropped the bar to 5 feet 5 ¼ inches—lower than the first jump-off, but high enough to give each woman a chance to break the tie and set a new record.

This time Jean Shiley made it. Then Babe ran toward the crossbar and leaped off the ground, kicking up her feet and rolling in midair as she went over the bar.

It was another tie—or was it? The judges huddled. According to Olympic rules then in effect, a high jumper had to clear the bar feet first. If the jumper went over the bar head first in a "dive," the jump was disqualified. The judges ruled that Babe had dived. The first-place gold medal went to Jean Shiley, the silver to Babe Didrikson.

This was another controversial ruling. Many of the reporters who were there felt that the decision was unfair, since Babe had been jumping the same way all afternoon, using a style called the Western roll, an acceptable jumping technique that had never been challenged until the Olympics. In 1932, however, most women used the classic scissors jump, which allowed less chance of fouling. The rule that the feet must cross the bar first held for women, but not for men, and was eliminated the following year. In recognition of the controversial nature of the decision, Babe was later made coholder with Jean Shiley of the high-jump world record set that day.

Babe sets a new world record in the high jump.

Despite the controversies, Babe emerged as the undisputed star of the women's games. She had broken world records in each event she entered and walked away with three medals—two gold and one silver. BABE BREAKS RECORDS EASIER THAN DISHES, announced one headline. Another said, BABE GETS PRAISE ON COAST: IS CALLED THE GREATEST WOMAN ATHLETE OF THE WORLD.

Babe was hailed as a conquering hero when she flew back to Dallas in a privately chartered American Airways transport escorted by fifteen United States Army planes, all paid for by Employers Casualty. Ten thousand people, including the mayor, were waiting at the airport to greet her. As she stepped from the plane, carrying a javelin in her hand, the Dallas Police Department band struck up "Hail to the Chief," and the city's fire chief escorted her to his gleaming red limousine, which was draped with hundreds of roses. Members of the Golden Cyclones formed an honor guard on either side of the open car as a festive ticker-tape parade set off through the streets of Dallas, with Babe perched on top of the back seat, waving to thousands of cheering fans who lined the route.

Babe's parents, her brother Ole, and her sister Lillie had driven up from Beaumont in Ole's battered old jalopy to help celebrate. By the time they arrived, the parade was about to start. When Babe spotted them, she

Homecoming: Babe's parents, Hannah (third from left) and Ole (far right), join the welcoming dignitaries in Dallas.

The conquering hero: Babe waves to her cheering fans as she rides through the streets of Dallas.

yelled, "Come on up here! Come on!" motioning for them to join her in the fire chief's car.

"[We] got up there with her," Lillie recalled, "and there were roses all over us, all *over* us. . . . We was so dirty and so *sweaty* when we finally found the landing field. We had two flat tires on the way there and the big shots, they was all looking at us country folks, but we didn't care. Babe didn't care. We had our parade through Dallas—confetti and scrap paper falling on the cars."

After the parade, Babe was feted at a luncheon attended by five hundred people at the Adolphus Hotel. During the speeches, when she was called to the microphone and invited to say something, she said simply, "I'm tickled to be back home," and sat down.

From Dallas, Babe flew to Beaumont for an equally stupendous welcome. Once again, thousands came to greet her, bands played, and crowds cheered as she rode through the streets in the Beaumont fire chief's red car, which was also draped in roses. This time, members of the Miss Royal Purple high-school teams marched as Babe's honor guard.

At a reception following the parade, Babe was presented with the key to the City of Beaumont. Her former Miss Royal Purple teammates gave her a silver cup with the inscription "We knew her when." A procession of dignitaries made speeches praising her, and her old friend, sportswriter Tiny Scurlock, told the guests, "She's the same swell kid she used to be."

The "worst kid on Doucette" had become, at the age of twenty-one, Beaumont's most illustrious citizen.

Practicing for an exhibition basketball game with the
Brooklyn Yankees, January 1933.

☆ ☆ ☆ *Seven* ☆ ☆ ☆

SHOW BUSINESS

*N*o one was surprised when the Associated Press poll of sports editors named Babe Didrikson as the outstanding Woman Athlete of the Year for 1932. "She is an incredible human being," wrote Grantland Rice, who had become her most ardent fan. "She is beyond all belief until you see her perform. . . . There is only one Babe Didrikson and there has never been another in her class—not even close to her class."

The press couldn't get enough of Babe. "She's capable of winning everything but the Kentucky Derby," one sportswriter quipped.

Babe was famous, but she still had to earn a living. After the Olympics, she returned to her clerical job at Employers Casualty. She wanted to maintain her amateur standing as an athlete so she could continue to compete, break records, and win gold medals.

The Illinois Women's Athletic Club tried to lure her away from Employers Casualty, offering her a similar office job for $300 a month if she would play for their teams. Babe was tempted, but she didn't want to leave Texas. When she told Homer R. Mitchell, the president of Employers

Casualty, about the Illinois offer, he agreed to match it. So Babe kept her job in Dallas at more than three times her previous pay and continued to play basketball for the Golden Cyclones.

With her new salary, she bought her first automobile, a shiny red Dodge coupe. She didn't realize it, but that car had trouble written all over it. A few weeks after she bought it, an advertisement appeared with a photo of Babe, a photo of a Dodge coupe just like hers, and an endorsement that quoted her as saying: "Speed—unyielding strength—enduring stamina—that's the stuff that makes real champions, whether they're in the athletic arena or in the world of automobiles."

Now, that just didn't sound like Babe. No one who knew her could believe that she had actually used those words. "If Babe said what the salesman said she said, I'll eat one of her javelins with mustard," wrote sports columnist Paul Gallico. But the ad appeared in newspapers across the country, and when officials of the Amateur Athletic Union saw it, they accused Babe of violating her amateur standing. It was against AAU rules to accept gifts or money for athletics or promotional work. Assuming that Babe had been paid for her endorsement, or had received the car free, the AAU suspended her from competition without a hearing. She was declared ineligible to play with the Golden Cyclones or to compete in future AAU track meets.

Babe was furious. She called the charges "a bunch of hooey." She insisted that she had purchased the car with her own money and hadn't been paid a penny for the ad. She wired the AAU, stating, "I positively did not give anyone authority to use my name or picture in any advertising matter."

The Dallas Dodge dealer and the advertising agency both came to her defense. The dealer reported that Babe had praised the car spontaneously in his showroom. He had told the agency about her enthusiasm, and that had become the basis for the advertisement.

The AAU wanted her to prove "beyond a doubt" that she had not consented to the endorsement. "I will do everything I can to be reinstated in the AAU and I don't want to turn professional," said Babe. "I have only played three years of basketball and I'm not ready to quit as an amateur."

Telegrams flew back and forth. Finally, the car dealer produced a let-

Benched: Babe sits on the sidelines between Colonel Melvin McCombs and Mrs. Henry Wood, team mother of the Golden Cyclones, after being suspended from competition by the Amateur Athletic Union.

ter that he had written to the advertising agency, proving that Babe had not authorized the disputed ad. The AAU backed down and reinstated her as an amateur.

But Babe felt that she had been treated unfairly. "Not until this last weekend," she told reporters, "did I realize what a terrifying business it is to maintain oneself as a member in good standing of the AAU." During the controversy, she'd had plenty of time to think about her future as an athlete. She had decided that now was the moment to cash in on her fame. Just before Christmas, she announced that she would give up her amateur standing and turn professional.

"The pressures got pretty heavy on me during the fall of 1932," she recalled. "People kept telling me how I could get rich if I turned professional. That big-money talk sounds nice when you're just a kid whose family never had very much."

A few days after resigning from the AAU, Babe turned up at the Detroit Auto Show with her sister Esther Nancy. She had been hired by the Chrysler Corporation to promote the same Dodge coupe that had caused all the trouble. The company felt "sorry about what had happened," she said, "and they wanted to make it up to me." Babe appeared daily at the Dodge display booth as a one-woman show. She chatted with people, signed autographs, and played her harmonica to attract a crowd.

Chrysler also asked an advertising executive named George P. Emerson to act as Babe's agent and arrange personal bookings for her. Emerson was the man who had created the controversial Dodge ad.

Newly turned professional, Babe is greeted at the Detroit Auto Show by Mayor Frank Murphy.

When the Auto Show ended, Emerson lined up a series of stage appearances for Babe on the RKO vaudeville circuit. Vaudeville stage shows, often paired with screenings of movies, were a popular form of entertainment in theaters all over the country. Babe's first booking was at the gigantic RKO Palace Theater in Chicago, where she would perform an eighteen-minute act. She was given top billing and the star's dressing room. "I had never done any kind of theatrical performance in my life," she wrote. "I thought I wasn't scared until we drove up to the theater the first morning, and I saw a crowd of people lined up down the block. I said, 'My Lord, I can't go through with this!'"

Her name in lights.

Babe was teamed with a piano player and comic named George Libbey. After he had warmed up the audience with an imitation of singer Eddie Cantor, Babe made her appearance from the theater lobby. She pranced down the center aisle wearing a Panama hat, a green swagger coat, and high-heeled platform shoes, looking as though she had just returned from a winter vacation in Florida. After swapping a few vaudeville gags with Libbey, Babe burst into song, belting out the lyrics to "I'm Fit as a Fiddle and Ready for Love." Then she kicked off her high heels, put on a pair of rubber-soled track shoes, and swept off her coat to reveal a red, white, and blue jacket and satin shorts.

A treadmill began moving on the stage. It was set in front of a black velvet backdrop with a big clock attached. Babe started jogging on the treadmill as the clock indicated her speed. At the same time, another woman began running on a similar treadmill. Babe jogged faster and faster, surging ahead and finally bursting through the tape—the winner again!

After that, Babe jumped a hurdle. Then she drove plastic golf balls into the audience. As a finale, she played familiar tunes on her harmonica, including "When Irish Eyes Are Smiling," "Begin the Beguine," and "Jackass Blues." She was a hit. Audiences loved the show and kept calling her back for encores.

During that week in Chicago, she did four or five shows daily. People formed long lines at the box office, standing patiently in the wintry Chicago winds. Emerson, her agent, had booked her for other RKO theaters in Manhattan and Brooklyn at a fee reported to be $2,500 a week, no small fortune in 1933. After that, she would tour the country with her act. But she was having second thoughts. She was spending all her time in the theater or in her hotel room. She talked it over with her sister Esther Nancy. "I don't want the money if I have to make it this way," she said. "I want to live my life outdoors." After only one week as a harmonica-playing vaudeville star, she canceled her advance bookings.

She wasn't sure what her next move would be. She was a professional now, but a professional what? At the time, only a handful of women had ever tried to make a living from sports. Athletic competition for women was confined almost entirely to amateur events, such as the track meets and basketball games sponsored by the AAU. There were few opportunities for serious competition open to women pros. Babe's only option as a professional was to show off her skills in exhibition games and promotional events.

She traveled to New York, where her agent had arranged a series of press interviews and exhibition matches. When she met with sportswriter Arthur Daley of the *New York Times,* she boasted that "no woman rivals me very closely as an athlete." When Daley asked, "What sport do you feel you're best at?" she replied, "I do everything best."

Babe made two highly publicized appearances in New York. She played an exhibition billiards game with Ruth McGinnis, the country's best female pool player, and lost. And she took part in her first professional basketball game, playing with a women's team called the Brooklyn Yankees against another women's team, the Long Island Ducklings, before

Practicing for an exhibition billiards game with Ruth McGinnis, women's professional pocket billiards champion.

a raucous crowd of two thousand fans in Brooklyn's Arcadia Hall. Babe's team won. When the game was over, she was presented with a real live Long Island duck. She took it back to her hotel room, kept it in the bathtub overnight, and shipped it home to her parents the next morning, air express.

She realized by now that her career as a professional wasn't leading anywhere. Her direction seemed aimless. She had saved enough money from her appearances to take some time off, so she decided to pursue a new interest. Babe had been playing golf on and off since her high-school days, when she had belonged to the Beaumont High golf club. Now she wanted to take up the game seriously. She felt that with professional coaching and enough practice, she could become an outstanding golfer.

In March 1933, she picked up her mother and her sister Lillie in Beaumont, and the three of them drove out to California in the Dodge coupe that had caused Babe so much trouble. They rented an apartment in Los Angeles, where Babe arranged to take daily lessons from a young golf pro named Stan Kertes.

As Kertes remembered, he was giving an exhibition at a driving range one evening when Babe and Lillie showed up to watch. "She was a warm and honest person and I liked her right away," he recalled. "She came up to me and said, 'Gee, you swing nice. Can you teach me that?' I knew her, of course, from the Olympics, and I said, 'Sure, we'll start now.'"

Babe's natural gifts as an athlete—her speed, strength, and stamina—had helped her excel in track and field. But golf demanded a different set of skills. It required such an intricate sense of touch, such finely tuned balance and control, that it could not be mastered without countless hours of practice. "Most things come natural to me," Babe once told a reporter, "and golf was the first that ever gave me much trouble."

She embraced her golf lessons with the same fierce determination she had brought to every other sport. She would arrive at the practice tee "at 9 in the morning . . . and often stay there till the place closed at midnight," Kertes remembered. "She hit ball after ball until her hands began to bleed, and I had to make her wear gloves and finally beg her to stop and rest. . . . I knew she had the makings of a champion."

With Kertes's help, Babe practiced golf diligently for six months. Finally her savings ran out, and she returned to Texas, where a job with

Golf pro Stan Kertes coaches Babe in Los Angeles.

Employers Casualty was always waiting. "Those people were wonderful to me," she recalled. "There must have been four or five times when I had to come back to them, and always there was a job for me at $300 a month."

That fall Babe's father fell ill and had to undergo an operation. Afterward, he wasn't able to work for quite some time. "It was up to me to earn some money," Babe recalled. "I wanted to make more than the $300 a month at Employers Casualty if I could."

She signed up with a sports promoter named Ray Doan, who organized a barnstorming basketball team called "Babe Didrikson's All-Americans." Along with Babe, the team included one or two other women and four men. They all piled into a car and set out on a five-month tour, visiting towns from Thief River Falls, Minnesota, to Fort Plain, New York, playing local basketball teams at night and driving on to the next town the following day.

"We played . . . a total of ninety-one games," recalled a teammate, "winning three-fourths of them and, twice, playing two games on the

Babe and her All-Americans basketball team.

same day in different towns and winning them both. We traveled in a seven-passenger sedan with a trailer for luggage, so we came to know each other very well."

Babe was the main attraction, the star, and because of her reputation, the All-Americans drew big crowds wherever they played. "She was very considerate," her teammate said, "and insisted whenever she was invited out that the team received an invitation too."

During the tour, Babe earned about $1,000 a month. At the time, women garment workers in New York were being paid as little as $5 for a fifty-hour work week. Babe sent most of her earnings home.

After the basketball season ended in 1934, Babe went to Florida to do some exhibition pitching in spring-training baseball games. She would usually pitch one inning, facing major-league teams like the Brooklyn Dodgers and the Boston Red Sox. It was a publicity stunt, but a profitable one for Babe, who was paid $200 for each one-inning appearance. She enjoyed meeting baseball greats like Dizzy Dean and Jimmy Foxx, and she began a lifelong friendship with her personal baseball hero, Babe Ruth. "I made a point of being introduced to him," she wrote, "because he was the original Babe."

After that, she went on the road again. This time she was booked to tour with a barnstorming all-male baseball team called the House of David, made up of men who belonged to a small Christian brotherhood based in Benton Harbor, Michigan. All the players sported full-grown beards. When the tour started, the *New York Evening Post* announced: FAMOUS WOMAN ATHLETE PITCHES FOR WHISKER TEAM.

The House of David team played more than two hundred games that summer, traveling from Fort Lauderdale, Florida, to Coeur d'Alene,

Babe poses for a gag shot with bearded members of the House of David baseball team.

Idaho, then touring through Canada. Babe wasn't the only big name on the team. Grover Cleveland Alexander, a former major-league pitcher, was also a star attraction, and they would each pitch for an inning or two. Babe, however, was the only woman.

She had no illusions about her role with the team. "I was an extra attraction to help them draw the crowd," she recalled. "I didn't travel with the team or anything. I hardly even got to know the players. I had my own car, and I had the schedule, and I'd get to whatever ballpark they were playing at in time for the game. I'd pitch the first inning, and then take off and not see them again until the next town."

It wasn't much of a life. There was no real challenge in those games, the traveling schedule was exhausting, and as a "girl athlete" appearing with all those bearded men, Babe was often the target of jokes and ridicule. "Sometimes in those early barnstorming days I wasn't sure if people were laughing with me or at me," she said.

But she was making loads of money, as much as $1,500 a month with the House of David, and that was what kept her going. When a reporter asked if she regretted giving up the thrills of amateur competition, Babe replied, "I like pro sports and will continue to like them—as long as the money keeps coming in. I guess we all like money."

Babe was supporting her parents now, and she was generous with everyone in her large family. She bought her father a new car, paid to remodel the family house, and was always sending expensive gifts home. Once, as a surprise on her mother's birthday, she had a new stove and refrigerator installed in the Didriksen kitchen. And when her sister Lillie got married, she paid for the wedding.

At a time when few women in America held high-paying jobs, Babe Didrikson was prospering. But she was paying a heavy price. "This freakish circus travel she went through after the Olympics was terribly hard on her, physically and emotionally, but spiritually, too," said her friend Ruth Scurlock. "She was really drained. Her father and mother were ill a lot of the time. She must have felt such enormous pressure, and yet she had to go through those demeaning travels and those ridiculous games."

A couple of years earlier, when Babe was winning Olympic gold medals, sportswriters had praised her as a teenage "wonder girl." Now that she was a tough and resourceful young woman trying to make a place for herself as a professional athlete, some reporters and members of the public regarded her as a travesty, a boastful has-been who bounced around the country trying to beat men at their own games. Babe's independence, her willingness to engage in just about any sport that caught her fancy and earned her money, seemed to touch a raw nerve among those who felt that the sports arena was a man's world and should stay that way.

Joe Williams, a columnist for the *New York World-Telegram*, used Babe as an excuse to attack all female athletes. He argued that women didn't belong in athletics, that they should spend their time looking for husbands. "It would be much better if [Babe] and her ilk stayed home, got themselves prettied up and waited for the phone to ring," wrote Williams.

Staying in shape.

Portrait of Babe around 1933.

Babe's detractors made snide remarks about her lean and wiry physique, her close-cropped hair, and her tailored clothes. They questioned her femininity, called her a tomboy who refused to grow up. Sportswriter Paul Gallico labeled Babe a "Muscle Moll," expressing his disdain for female athletes who did not fit his idea of proper feminine appearance or behavior.

Gallico argued that women should participate only in those sports that made them "look beautiful" and allowed them to wear "some pretty cute costumes." Acceptable sports, in his view, included archery, riding, and skating. Women should never engage in sports, like baseball, that made them perspire. "A girl just can't do those things and still be a lady," he wrote.

Gallico's opinions about female athletes were widely shared during the 1930s. Many people believed that so-called "feminine sports," in which women moved gracefully if they moved at all, were natural and healthy, while more strenuous activities were harmful because they weakened women for marriage and motherhood.

Babe herself was pointed out as an example of the dire effects that competitive sports could have on women. In Texas, physical education teachers posted signs on school bulletin boards saying, "DON'T BE A MUSCLE MOLL"—a warning to sports-minded girls.

Reporters were constantly putting Babe on the defensive with probing questions about her personal life. They wanted to know if she could cook, sew, and keep house, and whether she planned to marry. "People are always asking me 'Are you going to get married, Babe?' and it gets my goat," she said. "They seem to think I'm a strange, unnatural being summed up in the words 'Muscle Moll,' and the idea seems to be that Muscle Molls are not people. . . . I look forward to having a home and children just like anybody else, maybe more than some."

In later years, Babe was unwilling to talk about this phase of her life. She rarely mentioned her "Muscle Moll" days, saying, "My sports career began with golf." And she kept her Olympic track-and-field medals stuffed in a cigar box, not displayed openly with all her golf trophies.

*With her powerful swing, Babe scored an impressive 77 in
the qualifying round of the first golf tournament she entered.*

☆ ☆ ☆ *Eight* ☆ ☆ ☆

A NEW SPORT AND A NEW IMAGE

*B*abe looked back at her barnstorming days as "a mixed-up time for me. My name had meant a lot right after the Olympic Games, but it had sort of been going down since then. I hadn't been smart enough to get into anything that would really keep me up there."

That's why her thoughts had turned to golf. After taking lessons with Stan Kertes in Los Angeles, Babe had continued to practice her golf game as she barnstormed across the country with her All-Americans basketball team and the House of David baseball team. When the baseball season ended in the fall of 1934, she returned again to her office job in Dallas. Homer Mitchell, president of Employers Casualty, bought her a membership in the Dallas Country Club and paid for her golf lessons there with George Aulbach, the club pro.

By November 1934, Babe felt confident enough to enter her first golf tournament, the Fort Worth Women's Invitational. When reporters asked her how she thought she'd do in the qualifying round, she replied with typical bravado, "I think I'll shoot a seventy-seven." Amazingly, that's just

At her desk. Babe continued to work at Employers Casualty as she trained to compete in tournament golf.

what she did. She played her eighteen holes, and her score was an impressive 77. The next-best score was 82. Once again, Babe made headlines in the Texas newspapers: WONDER GIRL DEBUTS IN TOURNAMENT GOLF: TURNS IN 77 SCORE. "It was like 1932 all over again," Babe recalled.

Although Babe was eliminated in an early round of the tournament, she was encouraged by how well she had done. She hadn't expected to win a tournament her first time out. Her goal now was to play in the Texas State Women's Amateur Championship Tournament in the spring of 1935. If she could win *that* tournament against the best women golfers in Texas, she would establish herself as a major golf contender. She started practicing in earnest three months before the meet.

During the work week, she was up every morning at dawn and out on the course hitting golf balls from 5:30 until 8:30, when she had to leave for Employers Casualty. She worked until noon, ate a sandwich, then spent the rest of her lunch hour practicing her irons in her boss's carpeted office. She would stand in front of a mirror so she could watch her stance and chip balls into the boss's big leather chair, which had been moved safely away from the office window.

After lunch, she went back to work until 3:30. Then she was free to go to the Dallas Country Club for an hour's instruction with George Aulbach. Afterward, she'd drill on the different kinds of shots until it was too dark to practice any longer. "I'd hit balls until my hands were bloody and sore," she wrote. "I'd have tape all over my hands, and blood all over the tape."

The Texas State Women's Amateur Championship Tournament was being held at the River Oaks Country Club in Houston. Babe sent in her entry form, but at first it wasn't accepted. Tournament officials questioned her country-club membership, a requirement for all players. The real problem, however, was Babe's humble background. Golf was an exclusive country-club sport, played by wealthy society women. A golfer needed a set of clubs, private club membership, enough leisure time to play eighteen holes, and usually a caddie. Certain members of the Texas Women's Golf Association complained about Didrikson's lack of "social status." One member, Peggy Chandler, said, "We really don't need any truck-drivers' daughters in this tournament." Even so, Babe could not be barred from the tournament, because she was a member in good standing of both the Beaumont and Dallas country clubs.

A special ball-driving contest was scheduled for the day before the tournament opened. When Babe entered, several women withdrew, implying that they did not wish to compete against a "Muscle Moll." Stung by the hostility, Babe responded by clowning. At first, she purposely tapped ball after ball with an exaggerated "girlish" swing. Then she mustered her real power and let one fly. That ball rocketed more than 250 yards as caddies and spectators standing by cheered. She won the contest.

Like most tournaments at the time, this one employed the rules of match play, in which golfers compete one-on-one during each eighteen-hole round. The player finishing a hole with the fewest strokes wins that hole and scores one point. The player who wins the most holes is the winner of that round.

Babe was one of thirty-two women who qualified for the tournament. She won her first three rounds easily, advancing to the semifinals. That round, played on a rainy day, proved a lot tougher. At one point, the rain got so bad and the course so messy, Babe and her opponent had to stop playing for several hours until the weather cleared up.

From the beginning, Babe could outdrive most women golfers.

Babe won the match on the eighteenth hole with a spectacular twenty-foot putt. The ground was still soggy and the ball spurted water as it rolled across the green, approached the cup, seemed to pause at the lip—and dropped in. "Some women cried over the dramatic finish," wrote Bill Parker in his Associated Press story about the match. "Men hollered. Babe smiled and walked off the green—still America's wonder girl athlete and probably the most promising woman golf player in the United States."

In the final match, Babe's opponent was none other than Peggy Chandler, the Texas socialite who had turned up her nose at "truck-drivers' daughters." Chandler was a superb golfer, a former state champion. Babe was clearly the underdog. Their rivalry attracted a "gallery," or audience, of several hundred spectators who followed the golfers from hole to hole as they battled it out for the Texas championship. This was to be a marathon match played over thirty-six holes, eighteen holes in the morning and another eighteen that afternoon.

During the day-long contest, the lead shifted back and forth. At the twelfth hole, Babe led by five points. But Chandler closed the gap and by the twenty-fourth hole was three up (three points ahead). Didrikson rallied and evened the score on the thirty-third hole.

Suspense mounted as the gallery followed the golfers to the thirty-fourth hole. Chandler reached the green on her third shot; the ball was within two feet of the cup, and she seemed certain to take the hole in four.

Babe's first shot, a powerful 250-yard drive, had landed in a ditch. Her second shot skidded across the green, rolled onto a roadway used by

Babe and her chief rival, socialite Peggy Chandler, just before the final round of the Texas Women's Championship Tournament in Houston, April 1935.

trucks, and dropped into a wheel rut holding a puddle of rainwater from the day before. The top of the ball was just visible above the water.

Babe studied her third shot carefully, then took a sand wedge and swung. With a splash of mud and water, the ball leaped out of the rut, bounced across the green, and rolled into the hole! The gallery burst into whistles, cheers, and applause. Dozens of people rushed forward to congratulate Babe, and in the excitement, she was knocked facedown into the mud.

That turned out to be the deciding shot of the match. Babe was now one up with only two holes left to play. She wiped off the mud, tied Chandler on the thirty-fifth hole, then took the thirty-sixth to win the match and the women's championship of Texas.

"Staging a sensational finish," one newspaper reported, "the irrepressible Babe Didrikson Saturday rudely upset the polite circles of women's golf in Texas by defeating the veteran Mrs. Dan Chandler of Dallas two up to take the State title. . . . The tom-boy girl took up golf only two years ago."

Babe was on top of the world that day. "I was ready to shoot for the national championship," she wrote. But some members of the Texas Women's Golf Association were not pleased. After the tournament, one of them complained to the United States Golf Association (USGA) that Babe Didrikson was a professional athlete and did not belong in amateur golf. In Babe's view, she was a professional only in those sports governed by the Amateur Athletic Union, such as basketball and track and field. But she had never played as a professional in golf, which was governed by the rules of the USGA. She had applied for the Texas tournament as an amateur, and her application had been approved.

Even so, the USGA ruled against Babe, declaring her a professional because of her past appearances in baseball, basketball, and billiards exhibitions. She was barred from all amateur golf tournaments "in the best interest of the game."

Babe's friends and many fellow golfers spoke up in her defense, calling the USGA ruling a "bad mistake," a "big joke," a "dirty deal," and worse. Babe turned for advice to Bertha and R. L. Bowen, a wealthy Fort Worth couple who had befriended her and were influential in the Texas golf world. Bertha Bowen was convinced that Babe had a great future as a golfer. She suspected that the USGA ruling had more to do with Babe's social standing than her amateur standing. "I was just furious at those people who had been so cutting to her," she recalled. "The fact that she was poor and had no [acceptable] clothes did not mean she had to be ruled a professional."

The Bowens invited Babe to their home in Fort Worth. They consulted a lawyer on her behalf and sent a telegram to the USGA, protesting the ruling. The Beaumont Country Club, which Babe had represented as a golfer, petitioned the USGA to give her a full hearing, but to no avail. The ruling stood. As a result, Babe was now barred from every golf tournament except the Western Open, the only tournament then open to women professionals. All others were restricted to amateurs.

Bertha Bowen was an organizer of the Fort Worth Women's Invitational,

Golfer Bertha Bowen became one of Babe's closest friends and most influential supporters.

the amateur tournament that Babe had entered several months earlier. Bertha now used her influence to transform the Fort Worth Invitational into the Texas Women's Open, which became the second women's tournament to welcome professionals.

The new Texas Open was still several months away, so Babe decided to go back on the road. Since she had been declared a professional, she would start playing exhibition golf as a professional. She told a press conference that she would now be "a business woman golfer." She had signed a contract with a sporting goods company, P. Goldsmith Sons, to endorse their golfing equipment for a retainer of $2,500 a year. "As it all turned out, I'm very happy," she said. "My new job thrills me and I know that women's golf has a greater future in this country than men's golf. Golf is a game of coordination, rhythm and grace. Women have this to a much higher degree than men, as dancing shows."

With that, Babe teamed up with Gene Sarazen, one of the top male golfers of the day. During the summer of 1935, the two of them toured the country, staging exhibition matches against other twosomes before large and appreciative crowds. Along with her retainer from P. Goldsmith Sons, Babe earned between $250 and $500 for each match she played with Sarazen. "That was a lot of money in those days, but Babe was worth it," he recalled. "She was still a big draw because of the Olympics. . . . She was very congenial and always laughing. She had a gift for playing to the gallery. It just came naturally to her."

During a match, Babe would keep up a running banter with the spectators in the gallery, joking with them, kidding Sarazen, clowning between shots, and poking fun at herself. She would tell the crowd that the secret of her success was determination. "And my jaw helps plenty, too," she would add. "It's more like a Texas Ranger's jaw than anything else. And those Rangers were hot when the going got tough." Babe had always been a good talker, but it was during this tour that she polished her gifts as an off-the-cuff comedian. "I wasn't a finished golfer yet," she wrote. "But I could give the gallery some laughs."

Meanwhile, she was polishing her game. In between matches, she would ask Sarazen to work with her. "If I was going to be the best, I wanted to learn from the best," she wrote.

(RIGHT) Golfer Gene Sarazen toured the country with Babe during the summer of 1935.

(BELOW)

Letting one fly.

Sarazen taught her how to hit her way out of sand traps, water hazards, and other tricky situations. "She was very intense and wanted to learn," he recalled. "We'd play an eighteen-hole exhibition and then she'd go right back out and practice what she saw. . . . She learned all her golf by watching. She'd stand ten feet away from me and watch everything I did. Then she'd go out and practice it for hours."

That autumn Babe entered the first Texas Women's Open in Fort Worth, the tournament created by Bertha Bowen. But if the galleries were on Babe's side, some of the country-club golfers who competed against her were still hostile, and this time, their attitude seemed to unnerve Babe. She played poorly and was eliminated in an early round. "She used her bravado as a defense, but she really had a rough time in those early days of golf," Bertha said. "It's hard to break into society when they don't want you."

The Bowens invited Babe to stay at their luxurious home during the tournament. "That monkey," Bertha recalled, "she came for the Open and ended up spending three weeks with us." Bertha and her husband had lost an infant son not long before. They welcomed Babe into their lives with warmth and generosity and quickly formed a close bond with her. They were "like a godmother and godfather to me," said Babe.

"I was criticized by some of my friends for befriending Babe," Bertha recalled. "They'd ask me, 'Why are you fooling around with *that* girl?' It made me so mad. Sure, Babe could be crude, but around those ladies she was very timid. . . . She did want to do things right."

Babe had been snubbed not only because of her working-class background, but also because she seemed to defy conventional notions of proper feminine behavior. In an era when many people believed that women should be soft, submissive, and dependent, Babe Didrikson seemed all wrong. She was tough, resourceful, and independent. She was unmarried, self-supporting, and earning big money, a lot more than most men, and she resented reporters' constant questions about her marriage prospects. "Don't ask me whether or not I'm going to get married," she told Arthur Daley of the *New York Times*. "That is the first question women reporters ask. And that is why I hate those darn old women reporters."

Babe felt that she was always being put on the defensive, and she was getting tired of it. Early in her career she had tried to ignore the jokes and the rumors about her sexuality. She was in truth a vibrant and graceful young woman, very much at ease with herself, proud of her abilities, and she did not really want to conform. But now that she had decided on championship golf as her goal, her outlook began to change.

Because golf was played in a genteel country-club setting, it was considered a refined, ladylike game. Babe was moving in different social circles now. She realized that if she wanted to be accepted in the cultivated, upper-class world of women's golf, she would have to "fit in." Encouraged by Bertha Bowen, she began to shed her "Muscle Moll" image. She "was eager to be proper," Bertha recalled.

"I think the potential to make money attracted her to golf and the potential to become more of a celebrity, to be a real star," golfer Betsy Rawls has said. "Also, I think she picked golf because it was such a genteel sport. It was probably the most respectable sport for women there was in this country. Golfers were a very refined group. Being in that group gave Babe instant respectability in her eyes."

Babe let her hair grow out, had it waved, and borrowed some of Bertha's makeup and dresses. Then Bertha took her to the most exclusive shop in town and helped her pick out a stylish new wardrobe. The tomboy look vanished.

"Some writers have said that around this time a big change took place in me," Babe wrote in her autobiography. "Their idea is that I used to be all tomboy, with none of the usual girl's interests, and then all of a sudden I switched over to being feminine. Well, with almost any woman athlete, you seem to get that tomboy talk. It happens especially with girls who play things that generally aren't considered women's sports, like basketball and baseball, the way I did. . . . But I don't believe my personality has changed. I think anyone who knew me when I was a kid will tell you that I'm still the same Babe. It's just that as you get older, you're not as rambunctious as you used to be. You mellow down a little bit."

Whether Babe had truly "mellowed" or simply surrendered to the social demands of the golf world, the change in her appearance was striking. "I hardly knew Babe Didrikson when I saw her," wrote sports columnist Paul Gallico, who had coined the term "Muscle Moll." "Hair frizzed and she had

(LEFT) *This studio photo, taken around 1932–33, is inscribed to Babe's friend, sportswriter Tiny Scurlock.*

(BELOW) *Showing off her new image, Babe models an evening gown in a studio portrait taken around 1934–35.*

a neat little wave in it, parted and prettily combed, a touch of rouge on her cheeks and red on her lips. The tomboy had suddenly grown up."

Babe's new image was startling enough to turn some hard-boiled sportswriters into gushing fashion reporters. "Her figure is that of a Parisian model," wrote Henry McLemore of the United Press. "Her tweeds have the casual authority of New Bond Street and her ruby red nails were a creation of Charles of the Ritz. . . . Honestly, I had to look at her twice before I was sure she was the same Babe Didrikson that I had last interviewed at the women's national track and field championship in 1931."

Babe was twenty-four years old. Noting her transformation, some of her friends wondered if, far from being a "Muscle Moll," she had set her sights on finding a husband.

George Zaharias.

☆ ☆ ☆ *Nine* ☆ ☆ ☆

ROMANCE

*E*arly in 1936, Babe returned to California along with her parents, her sister Lillie, and her brother Arthur. She rented an apartment in Los Angeles and again took golf lessons from Stan Kertes. She was able to support the entire family on her income from P. Goldsmith Sons and the fees she earned playing exhibition matches. The rent on their "nice little" two-bedroom apartment near the Paramount movie studio was $27 a month.

Babe spent nearly two years in California, working to improve her golfing skills. By January 1938, she was ready to try her luck at a major tournament, the Los Angeles Open. While this was a regular competition on the men's circuit, there was no rule barring women. Babe became the first woman ever to qualify. "I knew I wasn't going to beat the top men pros," she wrote, "but I was still trying to establish myself as the greatest woman golfer."

At the opening round, she was teamed with two part-time golfers—C. Pardee Erdman, a Presbyterian minister and professor of religion, and George Zaharias, a professional wrestler. Babe had never heard of

Zaharias, but the local sports reporters certainly had, and they showed up in force.

"What an introduction George and I had!" Babe recalled. "One minute we were saying hello, and the next minute photographers were crowding around and calling for him to put wrestling holds on me. He put his arm around me, pretending to apply neck holds and stuff. I didn't mind at all."

Babe and George were both media hounds who knew how to play up to the press and have cameras point in their direction. They spent so much time clowning for the photographers, neither one did very well on the golf course that day. Reverend Erdman beat them both. "We kept joking with the preacher that maybe he'd just have to up and marry us, we were getting along so well," George recalled.

That night George invited Babe to join him for dinner. The next day they played the second round of the tournament together, and while neither qualified for the third round, they agreed to go out dancing. "I love to dance," she told him. They went to a night spot called the Cotton Club, where the club artist sketched their portraits in charcoal. George autographed his portrait and gave it to Babe. She autographed hers and gave it to him.

"It sort of built up from there," Babe recalled. "George took to calling me 'Romance,' and when I wrote a note to him I'd sign it 'Romance.'" We were going together real steady, except that he had to be away a lot to wrestle, and I had my golf bookings."

Babe was twenty-six when they met. George was twenty-nine, a strapping six-footer with shoulders as wide as a doorway, "husky and black-haired and handsome," as Babe described him. He had an easy smile, a booming laugh, and ears crushed like cauliflowers from his years in the wrestling ring. They found they had a lot in common. Both came from poor immigrant families that had struggled to get established in America. And they were both tough and resourceful athletes who had fought their way to recognition and success. From the time they met, Babe Didrikson and George Zaharias seemed to understand and admire each other.

George Zaharias, born Theodore Vetoyanis, was the son of immigrants from Greece who had settled on a hardscrabble farm near Pueblo, Colorado. As a youngster, he labored on the family farm and in a Pueblo steel

George and Babe on the golf course.

mill alongside his father, which "must have helped to develop those tremendous muscles of his," Babe noted. Still a teenager, he dropped out of school and joined a traveling circus as a roustabout. Eventually he wound up in Chicago, where he saw a sign outside a gym saying: WRESTLERS WANTED, 1 DOLLAR A DAY.

Professional wrestling at the time was less a sport than a form of vaudeville performance art. Wrestlers who took part needed acting ability as well as athletic agility. Young Theodore Vetoyanis had both. Changing his name to George Zaharias so he would not embarrass his family, he quickly became a star on the professional wrestling circuit.

Wrestling matches were designed as crowd pleasers. They featured a hero who always won and a scowling villain who lost. Zaharias played the role of the cowardly wrestling villain who fouled, cheated, and gouged before the tables were turned. Howling and begging for mercy, he would finally go down to mock defeat, cringing, pleading, and weeping. It was said that George Zaharias could weep real tears in the wrestling ring.

George Zaharias (right), "The Weeping Greek from Cripple Creek," in the wrestling ring.

Eventually he was billed as "The Weeping Greek from Cripple Creek" (a town not far from Pueblo). When he wrestled in Los Angeles, movie stars would come to see him perform in the ring. They would always sit up close, so that they could watch George act.

By the time Babe met George in 1938, he was a wrestling celebrity and a wealthy man. Like Babe, he supported his parents. He had built them a fine home, set up two brothers-in-law in business, and paid for the educations of his two younger brothers. He was like Babe, also, in his expansive self-confidence, in his boisterous vitality and zest for life.

As far as anyone could recall, Babe had never had a serious romance. Somewhere along the line she had learned to dance, but she had never shown much interest in boys, except as competitors to be bested in sports events. But she was having a romance now, and with a good-looking man who was a sports star in his own right. She brought George home to introduce him to her family. As he was getting ready to leave, Babe's mother reached up, patted him on the cheek, and said, "My Babe, she likes you."

That summer Babe entered the Western Women's Open, which was being held in Colorado Springs, near George's hometown of Pueblo. George took her out to meet his parents. "His mother didn't speak too much English," Babe wrote, "but she and I got along fine just the same." Babe was edged out in the semifinal round of the Western Women's Open, but "that particular summer, losing a golf match didn't seem to matter as much to me as it ordinarily did."

A month later, on July 22, 1938, Babe Didrikson and George Zaharias announced their engagement. "We're very much in love," Babe told reporters. Soon afterward, they visited Beaumont, where Babe introduced George to her old friends Ruth and Tiny Scurlock. "We were so excited," Ruth recalled. "We knew George because he had wrestled in Beaumont many times. Babe had this big ring and she was so delighted. . . . She seemed to like to play the little woman, to have someone there to protect her and defend her. It was a role she had never played before. She was so happy that night."

They wanted to have a wedding with both families present, but George's wrestling matches and Babe's golfing appearances kept both of them on the move. "We could never seem to work out a date for the wedding," Babe wrote. In December, they both happened to be in St. Louis together, and as Babe put it, "George got real stern with me. He said, 'We're going to get married this week or call the deal off.' I said, 'It's a deal. Let's go!'"

"We had been happy and we were not under any pressure," George recalled, "but I wanted her to be mine, and I told her so. And she said, 'If that's the way you want it, we'll do it.'"

George and Babe were married by a justice of the peace on December 23, 1938, at the St. Louis home of a wrestling promoter named Tom Packs. Baseball star Leo Durocher of the Brooklyn Dodgers was George's best man, and Leo's wife, Grace, stood up for Babe. She helped Babe pick out her wedding outfit, a blue dress and blue hat. Several friends from the St. Louis area attended. "It was a very nice affair," said Babe.

George slips the wedding ring on Babe's finger.

Because of their many professional commitments, she and George had to delay their honeymoon until the following spring, and even then, they both continued to perform. They took a boat trip to Australia, where George had lined up a grueling schedule of wrestling matches for himself and golf exhibitions for Babe. She played on courses all over the country, competing against Australia's best golfers and winning praise from the press as a "magnificent specimen of athletic womanhood. . . . The plain fact is that Miss Didrikson is a vastly better golfer than . . . any other woman we have seen." On the way home, Babe played exhibition matches in New Zealand and Hawaii. All together, they were gone for six months.

Back in California in the spring of 1939, Babe had to do some heavy thinking about her future as a golfer. "Here I'd been practicing all the time, and developing this fine golf game, and about all I could do was play exhibition matches. I wasn't getting a chance to show whether I was the best woman player, because I was barred from practically all of the women's tournaments as a professional."

Only two tournaments were open to her, the same two as in 1935—the Western Women's Open and the Texas Women's Open. "What I really wanted in golf was to compete and win championships," she wrote. The only way she could do that was to get her amateur standing back. There just weren't enough opportunities for a woman pro.

According to the rules of the United States Golf Association, Babe could apply for reinstatement as an amateur if she gave up all forms of playing for pay for a period of three years. Before her marriage, she had depended on her earnings as a professional athlete to support herself and her family. Now she had George, whose success as a wrestler and a shrewd business investor had made him a millionaire. His income was more than enough to carry Babe and her dependent family through the three-year waiting period. "I had a great career of my own," he told an interviewer. "I found myself dedicating myself to her and letting her do what she wanted."

In January 1940, Babe canceled all her professional contracts and appearances and began her three-year waiting period. "I'd much rather be competing for the fun of the game than just playing for money," she told the USGA. She and George rented a house with a yard in West Los Angeles. Babe planted rosebushes, bought a sewing machine, and made curtains, slipcovers, and bedspreads. George, meanwhile, decided to retire from active wrestling and become a full-time sports promoter, organizing wrestling matches and managing his wife's career. "I was sweetheart, husband, manager, adviser," he said, "but they weren't jobs. It was a chance for me to be with the greatest girl in the world."

Babe practiced her golf game regularly. In 1940, she entered the two tournaments she was eligible for—the Western Women's Open and the Texas Women's Open—after announcing that she would not accept any prize money. She surprised everyone by winning both tournaments. "I could hardly wait for my amateur standing to return, so I could begin going after all the top championships," she wrote.

While waiting, she decided to master tennis. "I wanted to see whether I couldn't work my way to the top in one more sport," said Babe. She took lessons at the Beverly Hills Tennis Club from Eleanor Tennant, a top pro, and practiced with her usual intensity, playing sixteen or seventeen sets a day. Soon she could beat Tennant, her teacher. She practiced against some of the best players in the country and often beat them.

After a year and a half of lessons, she was ready to compete in her first tennis tournament. In the fall of 1941, she sent in her entry for the Pacific Southwest Championships, sponsored by the United States Lawn Tennis Association (USLTA), but her application was rejected. According to the USLTA's rules, anyone who had played any sport as a professional was barred forever from competition in amateur tennis. Babe was informed that she would never be eligible to compete in events sponsored by the USLTA.

"Once I knew I could never compete in tournaments, that took the fun out of tennis for me," she wrote in her autobiography. "It's not enough for me just to play a game. I have to be able to try for championships. So I quit tennis cold. I still have my rackets, but I haven't touched them from that day to this."

She took up bowling, a sport that did allow her to compete as an amateur. Now she spent hours every evening in bowling alleys. She took lessons from several pros and bowled on some of the top teams in the Los

*Babe takes
tennis lessons
from Eleanor
Tennant.*

Angeles area. A sportswriter called her "one of the best women bowlers in Southern California."

But she still had her sights set on golf, "my favorite sport." Occasionally there was a tournament she was allowed to enter during her three-year waiting period, but mostly she kept her game up by playing three or four practice rounds a week.

☆　☆　☆

Aiming for a strike.

The sports scene in America changed abruptly after Japanese warplanes bombed the U.S. naval base at Pearl Harbor, Hawaii, on December 7, 1941. The nation entered World War II, mobilizing to fight Japan in the Pacific and Germany and Italy in Europe. Many golf tournaments and other sports programs were suspended or curtailed for the duration. Babe and George both placed their skills and reputations at the service of the war effort. George organized wrestling exhibitions that toured American military bases all over the world. Babe helped sell war bonds and raise money for armed services charities by playing exhibition matches with famous golfers such as Ben Hogan and Sam Snead, and with Hollywood celebrities, including comedian Bob Hope and singer Bing Crosby.

Her matches with Hope and Crosby turned out to be among the sporting highlights of the war. The three of them would clown and joke as they played—a comic golf-course routine that kept the spectators in the gallery laughing and the press cameras clicking. Hope's favorite line was "There's only one thing wrong about Babe and myself. I hit the ball like a girl and she hits it like a man." Babe was flattered by the joke, because in truth, she could easily outdrive both Hope and Crosby.

Celebrity golf. Crooner Bing Crosby (left), Babe Didrikson Zaharias, and comedian Bob Hope watch Patty Berg tee off at a wartime exhibition match.

Her special crowd pleaser in those wartime exhibition matches was an assortment of dazzling trick shots she had mastered during her tours with Gene Sarazen. She would set up five balls on the tee and hit them so rapidly one after another that the fifth ball would be in the air before the first one hit the ground. Then she would stack up two balls and hit the bottom one down the fairway while the top ball popped up into her pocket. Finally, she would lay a row of golf clubs down on the green and putt the ball so that it jumped over each club as if by magic and then dropped into the hole.

On January 21, 1943, Babe's three-year waiting period ended, and she regained her amateur standing with the USGA. But America was still at war, and she had few chances to compete as an amateur. Most of the big tournaments had been canceled. Babe played in numerous charity matches and in small local tournaments. And she spent many unpublicized hours during the war as a volunteer, teaching disadvantaged and troubled children to play ball, swim, and golf.

It wasn't until the summer of 1944 that she had a chance to enter a major tournament, the Western Women's Open, which she had won as a professional back in 1940. She won again in 1944, her first important vic-

Babe points to her winning score at the Western Women's Open, June 1944.

tory as an amateur. A year later, in June 1945, she defended her Western Women's Open title, hoping to capture her third championship, something that no golfer had ever done.

The tournament was held that year in Indianapolis, Indiana. Babe got off to a great start, winning her opening match easily. That evening, George called with alarming news. Babe's mother, Hannah, had been rushed to a Los Angeles hospital after suffering a heart attack. She was in critical condition. Babe wanted to fly to Hannah's bedside, but George urged her to wait, telling her, "Your momma wants you to finish the tournament." Babe's sister Esther Nancy was with Hannah at the hospital, and she said the same thing.

Babe tried to return to Los Angeles anyway, but because of wartime travel priorities, she could not get a seat on any plane or train out of Indianapolis that day. The next day she played her quarterfinal match and won. That night Esther Nancy called to tell her that Hannah had died. "I've got to get back," Babe cried. "You go ahead and win that tournament," said Esther Nancy. "That's the way Momma would want it."

Again, Babe tried desperately to get transportation out of Indianapolis, but without success. Airlines had their scarce seats reserved for Washington VIPs and military brass, trains were filled with troops, and Babe didn't rate a high enough priority. She went ahead, played tearfully in the semifinals, and won again. "A lot of times I'd have to step away and wipe my eyes before I could putt," she remembered. "What kept me going was that I felt I was playing for Momma now."

That night Babe asked two fellow golfers, Peggy Kirk Bell and Marge Row, to have dinner with her in her hotel room. She had met them just a few days earlier, when the tournament opened. Both women knew her mother had died, and they expected her to default. "We didn't know what to expect that night," Bell recalled. "Babe just sat there and played her harmonica. She played for hours. I didn't think we'd ever eat. She didn't speak, she just kept playing the harmonica. I guess it was her way to overcome sadness."

The next day Babe went out for the finals against Dorothy Germain, the golfer she had beaten in the deciding match of the same tournament the year before. "I was really inspired," she wrote. In the morning round

Babe manages a victory smile as she hugs the Western Women's golf trophy for the third time in her career. Her finalist opponent, Dorothy Germain, looks on. The next day, Babe flew to Los Angeles for her mother's funeral.

she set a new women's record for the course with a score of 72. Then she won the afternoon round to take the championship, becoming the first woman to win it three times.

At five o'clock the next morning, she was notified that a seat on a plane was finally available. During her flight to the West Coast, she was bumped three times by priority passengers, and she had to wait for hours at airports in Kansas City, Albuquerque, and Phoenix before getting on connecting flights. She reached Los Angeles two days after leaving Indianapolis.

Her father had died of cancer two years earlier. At the time, Babe remembered, "The rest of us were crying and everything, but I noticed that Momma wasn't. I couldn't understand it, as much as she and Poppa had meant to each other for so many years. I said, 'Momma, why aren't you crying?' She said, 'Babe, if I cried, then you children would start fussing over me. I want you to cry for Poppa.'"

Now the time had come to weep for Hannah. The family had held up the funeral until Babe could get there, and they drove her from the airport directly to the funeral home. *"Poor Momma!"* Because Babe had always been so close to her mother, the loss seemed almost more than she could bear. "I never could cry too easy when I was a kid," she wrote, "but when I saw Momma there that day in 1945, I really broke down. The others just left me alone in the chapel to cry."

Hannah Didriksen was buried on June 26, 1945. It was Babe's thirty-fourth birthday.

Signing autographs at the British Women's Amateur tournament in Gullane, Scotland, June 1947.

☆ ☆ ☆ *Ten* ☆ ☆ ☆

SUPERMAN'S SISTER

*W*orld War II ended with Japan's unconditional surrender on August 14, 1945. In the United States, the sports world gradually returned to its prewar schedule, and Babe Didrikson Zaharias finally had her chance to compete for the top women's golf championships.

That autumn, Babe won her second Texas Women's Open title. Then she defeated golfer Betty Jameson in a series of widely publicized challenge matches at Los Angeles and San Antonio. In December, the Associated Press poll of sports editors voted her Woman Athlete of the Year, the same honor she had received after the 1932 Olympics.

"This was the first time I'd been picked since then," she wrote. "During all those years in between, what with my troubles over professionalism and everything, I hadn't been able to compete enough to establish whether I was the No. 1 woman athlete."

As the 1946 season got underway, Babe told an interviewer, "I want to establish the longest winning streak in the history of golf." After saying that, she lost a match when she was edged out of the Western Women's

Open in June. But "that was the last losing I was going to do for a long time."

Beginning with the Trans-Mississippi Women's Amateur in Denver in August 1946, Babe embarked on a string of victories unmatched by any other golfer, male or female, amateur or professional. She entered virtually every major tournament, competing against the world's finest women golfers, and for more than a year she did not lose a single match. By the end of 1946, she had won five consecutive tournaments, including the National Women's Amateur championship. Once again, the Associated Press voted her Woman Athlete of the Year.

In 1947, she continued to pile up victories. Babe was hot. By the middle of the year, she claimed a winning streak of fifteen tournaments in a

Working on her winning streak.

row, a record no golfer had ever approached. "She won everything in sight," said Peggy Kirk Bell. "Babe was so confident, she was hard to compete against."

Wherever she played, she attracted large crowds, and even in the heat of competition, she would take time to entertain the galleries with trick shots and wisecracks. When one of her powerful drives sailed out of bounds, she'd turn to the crowd and explain, "I hit it straight but it went crooked." When she missed a short putt, she'd say, "I feel like nuts and bolts rattling together."

"I just love a gallery," she wrote. "It bothers some athletes to have people always crowding around them. I wouldn't feel right if the people weren't there. Even in a tournament, I like to kid around with the gallery."

As summer began, she was ready to take a break. Babe and George had recently moved to Denver, where they bought a beautiful old English-style house, the first house they had ever owned. Babe wanted to relax and enjoy her new home. "I was really ready to go home and see my flowers and work around the house and garden," she wrote. But George persuaded her otherwise. He urged her to go over to Scotland and enter the prestigious British Women's Amateur, known officially as "The Ladies Amateur Golf Championship Tournament."

"You need something like that to top off your [winning] streak," George said. No American had won the British Women's Amateur since the tournament began in 1893. Babe had a chance to be the first. She couldn't resist.

"There was never any event that was more important for me in sports than the British Women's Amateur golf championship in 1947," she wrote. The tournament was to be held in June at Gullane, Scotland. George had promised to make the trip with Babe, but at the last minute, he begged off. His commitments as a sports promoter made it difficult for him to be away that long. So Babe went alone. She had never been to Europe before.

She sailed across the Atlantic to Southampton, England, then rode the train to London, where she was to catch another train to Scotland's capital city, Edinburgh. By the time she reached the London station, however, the train to Scotland was jammed. Every seat had been taken. Unrecognized, she had to stand in the aisle with her luggage for most of the ten-hour trip. "Whenever anybody left their seat for a few minutes, I'd go sit there until they came back," she wrote.

In Edinburgh, a private car was waiting at the station to take her to Gullane, the picturesque old village where the tournament was being held. Babe's winning streak had been widely reported in both American and British newspapers, and the people of Gullane were curious to meet her. As she walked along the town's cobbled streets from the North Berwick Inn, where she was staying, to the Gullane golf course, people would call out greetings and sometimes invite her into their cottages for tea. "Hello, Mrs. Zaharias," they would say, and Babe would reply, "Howdy," in her best Texas twang. She told the reporters who seemed to follow her everywhere, "I wish you'd ask everybody just to call me Babe." And that's what people started to do.

She had arrived several days early so she could familiarize herself with Gullane's windswept seaside golf course, which was inhabited by wandering flocks of sheep that kept the grass cropped. As a special courtesy, the course provided Babe with a white-coated attendant who walked along in front of her and scooped up sheep droppings. Local golfers had to manage that task on their own.

Across from two of the fairways was a street lined with big old houses. When Babe practiced, people would stand or sit at the windows of those houses, watching her. She always waved, and they would wave back. One family came over and invited her to dinner. "I went there a couple of times, and became good friends with them," she wrote.

She wasn't prepared for the unpredictable Scottish weather, which turned raw and wet soon after she arrived. She had packed for summer. Postwar rationing was still in effect in Britain, and Babe had no ration coupons to buy warmer clothes. When she mentioned her discomfort to reporters, stories ran in the local papers. Overnight, gifts of warm clothing began to arrive at the North Berwick Inn, and before long, the lobby of the inn was stacked high with bundles.

She rummaged through them and picked out a World War II jumpsuit, "one of those things the British air-raid workers used to wear," and a pair of light-blue corduroy slacks. From then on, she'd take the jumpsuit and slacks out to the course with her, carrying them in her golf bag. If the weather turned chilly, she'd pull on the jumpsuit. If it got really cold or rainy, she'd slip the slacks over it. Those slacks—or "slocks," as the Scots called them—became known as Babe's "lucky pants."

Ninety-nine women entered the tournament. Starting on a Monday morning, pairs of competitors chosen by lot would play two eighteen-hole matches a day, one in the morning and one in the afternoon, with the loser of each match being eliminated. By Thursday, the two remaining players would compete in a thirty-six-hole final.

Babe won her first match easily, but she was puzzled by the silence of the gallery that followed the players around the course. From time to time she would hear someone murmur, "Well played," or "Fine shot," and

Wearing her lucky slacks, Babe drives a long one at the Gullane links in Scotland.

when she clinched the match on the twelfth hole, those watching applauded politely. Obviously, the crowd was much more reserved than American spectators. Babe told Helen Holm, one of the tournament marshals, "I wish these people would just holler and enjoy themselves the way the crowds do back home." Holm explained that the Scottish tradition was for the gallery to be very quiet so as not to disturb the players.

That wasn't what Babe was used to, and she wanted "to loosen up those galleries if I could." During her afternoon match that day, she began to kid around with the crowd, telling them they could make all the noise they wanted. It wouldn't bother her, she promised; it would just make her play better. She won that match on the sixteenth hole. Then she and her opponent agreed to give the crowd an extra show by playing the two remaining "by-holes." While this was common practice in American tournaments, it wasn't usually done in Scotland, where tradition dictated that play stopped once a winner had been decided.

Since Babe was a visiting American, they went ahead. She decided to show off some of her trick shots. On the seventeenth tee, she slyly placed a kitchen match behind her ball. When she teed off, the match flared up with a loud pop, "like a small cannon being fired." The gallery gasped in surprise, then started to laugh, then watched in amazement as the ball sailed at least 250 yards and landed in a sand trap just off the green.

At the sand trap, Babe pulled another stunt. She set a second ball on top of the one in the sand and swung gently. Ordinarily, the bottom ball would fly onto the green while the top one jumped into her pocket. This time, as luck would have it, one ball did land in her pocket while the other skipped across the green and dropped right into the hole!

By now, the crowd was in an uproar. On the eighteenth green, Babe made her last shot by turning around, bending over, and putting the ball backward between her legs into the hole as the crowd broke into cheers and applause. Afterward, she spent nearly an hour signing autographs.

The next day tournament officials posted a sign on the clubhouse bulletin board reading, PLEASE DO NOT PLAY THE BY-HOLES. "So I didn't do that anymore," Babe wrote. "But those crowds got bigger and friendlier every day. They sounded almost like the crowds at home by the end of the tournament."

The British had never seen anyone quite like her. By the time she reached the semifinals, her gallery had grown to an enthusiastic crowd of some eight thousand people. In that match she faced Jean Donald, the Scottish champion and the woman considered most likely to defeat Babe. Everyone expected a close contest. But Babe was in top form that afternoon. "She must be Superman's sister," a spectator exclaimed after Babe had whacked one of her powerful drives. She won the semifinal match by a lopsided score, seven up with five holes to go.

Babe poses with Scottish golf champion Jean Donald, her opponent in the semifinal match at Gullane.

In the final, a thirty-six-hole match, Babe faced British golfer Jacqueline Gordon. The weather that morning was warm and sunny for a change. Babe put on a light sweater and skirt and left her jumpsuit and blue corduroys behind. Midway through the first eighteen-hole round, however, the weather turned windy and chilly. Babe began to shiver. "Pretty soon I was wishing for my cold-weather stuff," she wrote. "I didn't burn up the course during that morning round the way I had in practically all my other matches." At the end of the morning round, the match stood even. As the golfers broke for lunch, people in the gallery called out, "Babe, go get your slocks on! Go get your slocks on!"

When she returned for the afternoon round, she was dressed more warmly in her jumpsuit and her blue corduroys, her "lucky pants." They must have been exactly that. Babe broke the tie on the first hole and stayed ahead of Jacqueline Gordon for the rest of the match. She captured the British Women's Amateur championship on the thirty-second hole, five up with four holes left to play.

The gallery broke into applause that lasted "for fifteen minutes," according to Babe. She was elated. When photographers asked her to go around to the front of the clubhouse for pictures, she broke into a sprint, hurdled a brick wall, and danced a highland fling.

"Surely no woman golfer has accomplished in a championship what Mrs. Zaharias has achieved in this one," declared the *Manchester Guardian*, a leading British newspaper. "She has never had to go beyond the 16th green and she has lost only four holes in six rounds. . . . She is a crushing and heart-breaking opponent."

Before heading home, Babe spent a few days playing some of Scotland's legendary golf courses, including historic St. Andrews. Her high spirits and spectacular golf game had endeared her to sports fans all over Britain, and when her train left Edinburgh for London, the station platform was crowded with hundreds of admirers singing "Auld Lang Syne." This time, Babe had a reserved seat on the train.

She sailed back to New York on the *Queen Elizabeth*. As the great liner approached New York City, a tugboat jammed with reporters, photographers, and newsreel cameramen came out to meet the ship and greet the first American woman to win the British Women's Amateur champi-

The winner: Babe becomes the first American-born golfer to capture the British Women's Amateur championship.

onship. George was standing up front, gripping the tugboat's rail, and when Babe spotted him, she waved and hollered. Then she put two fingers in her mouth and whistled. At that moment, the whistle on the *Queen Elizabeth* let out a blast. Later, George told Babe, "Honey, I could hear your whistle above the *Queen Elizabeth*'s."

Babe and George spent several days in New York, celebrating her victory and giving interviews. Then they flew to Denver, their new home, where a festive parade and reception awaited them. The parade featured gaily decorated floats, each one representing one of the sports Babe had played—basketball, baseball, javelin throwing, hurdling, and the rest. Babe rode on the last float, surrounded by roses and waving to the crowds as an airplane above spelled out "Hi Babe" in skywriting.

Mayor Quigg Newton of Denver hands Babe a silver trophy while George wraps his arm around a 14-foot, 250-pound key to the city.

At City Hall, she was greeted by the governor of Colorado and the mayor of Denver, who presented her with a giant key to the city while fifty thousand onlookers roared their approval. The key was more than twice as tall as George and weighed 250 pounds. However, George, by this time, weighed even more. And while he didn't have to carry the key home, he did show the crowd that he could lift it off the ground.

Babe Didrikson Zaharias shows off her pitching arm to the original "Babe," baseball legend Babe Ruth.

☆ ☆ ☆ *Eleven* ☆ ☆ ☆

"OKAY, BABE'S HERE!"

*T*wo weeks after she returned from Scotland, Babe added another notch to her winning streak with a lopsided victory in the Broadmoor Match Play Tournament at Colorado Springs. By now, all sorts of offers were pouring in from advertisers and promoters. "It got to the point where I stood to make a fast half-million dollars," Babe wrote. "It's pretty hard to say you don't want the kind of money I was being offered."

She couldn't resist, and neither could George. Together, they drove back to New York and signed up with sports promoter Fred Corcoran. On August 14, 1947, Babe announced at a press conference that she was turning professional again. "It nearly killed me to throw over the amateur standing I'd struggled so hard to get, but I couldn't see any choice," she said.

Fred Corcoran was director of the Men's Professional Golf Association and the agent for some of the biggest sports celebrities of the time, including golfer Sam Snead and baseball stars Ted Williams and Stan Musial. "They were great guys," he recalled, "but when it came to getting headlines, Babe had them all beat. She had a fantastic feel for publicity."

Babe was a sports promoter's dream, and Corcoran immediately capitalized on her soaring popularity. That summer, he booked Babe at several major-league ball parks, where she put on a pregame act that included pitching during batting practice, taking a few cuts at the plate, then hitting golf balls into the outfield.

At Yankee Stadium one evening, she called for a glove and stepped in at third base as the home team took the field for infield drill. "Her barnstorming days were back!" Corcoran recalled. "She was hobbled somewhat by her skirt, but that didn't faze her. She ripped it up the front and went back to scooping up ground balls and firing them across to first base. The crowd went wild."

Babe at bat during a pregame exhibition at Yankee Stadium, June 1948. Afterward, she drove golf balls into the outfield. Note her golf bag and club in the foreground.

As a golfer, Babe began to play exhibition, charity, and professional matches all over the country. Corcoran signed her to a lifetime contract with the Wilson Sporting Goods Company, which marketed a line of Babe Zaharias golf equipment. She also renewed her old partnership with the P. Goldsmith Sons sporting goods company, endorsing their products. She published a popular book of golfing tips. And she signed with a dress manufacturer to "co-design" a line of women's golfing outfits that would carry her name.

In October 1947, Babe returned to Fort Worth for the Texas Women's Open, her first golf tournament since again turning professional. She had won the Texas Open three times in the past, but this year the grueling schedule arranged by Corcoran had taken a toll. She was edged out in the quarterfinals by a young amateur named Betty Mims White, snapping her winning streak. At this point Babe claimed seventeen consecutive victories—the longest winning streak in the history of golf.

Furious with herself for losing at Fort Worth, she came roaring back in her next tournament, winning the Hardscrabble Women's Open at Little Rock, Arkansas. Her spectacular seventy-two-hole score of 293, an average of 73 plus per round, set a world's record for women's tournament medal play. Even so, Babe's loss at Fort Worth stuck in her craw, and for years afterward she brooded about it. "I honestly believe that if I had squeaked through in the Texas Women's Open, I'd have gone on and stretched my winning streak to twenty-five or thirty tournaments," she wrote.

In any case, 1947 was another banner year for Babe, highlighted by her stunning victory in Scotland and crowned by her record-breaking performance at Little Rock. For the third year in a row, the Associated Press voted her Woman Athlete of the Year.

Meanwhile, she was constantly on the go. "The fees [for golf exhibitions] were good," she wrote, "but we probably booked too many of them. One month there were seventeen nights that I was on a plane. I'd play one place, then go to the airport to fly to the next place. That grind began to wear me down physically, although it was years before I'd admit it."

With her exhibition matches, endorsements, and personal appearances, she was making more than $100,000 a year at a time when a physical education teacher earned about $3,500. Her golf game had never been better. But she found herself facing the same problem that had been so frustrating a few years earlier: Babe craved competition. As a professional, however, she had little chance to enter major tournaments and go after championships. There were a few more tournaments open to women pros than in the 1930s, but not nearly enough to challenge a golfer like Babe.

She felt that there should be a professional golf association for women, just as there was for men, an idea enthusiastically supported by Fred Corcoran, her agent. A group called the Women's Professional Golf Association had been founded a few years earlier but had disbanded after sponsoring a single tournament. Corcoran learned that a new organization would not be permitted to use the same name as the old one. They'd have to come up with something else. "Well, okay," he recalled, "we thought, in England they call them 'ladies' and in a way it sounded classier than 'women.' We decided to call our tour the 'Ladies Professional Golf Association.'"

In January 1949, Babe and George Zaharias met with Fred Corcoran and golfer Patty Berg at the Venetian Hotel in Miami, Florida, and drew up the charter for the Ladies Professional Golf Association (LPGA). Berg volunteered to be the group's first president. They believed that with a formal organization working to promote the game, more women golfers would want to compete as professionals.

During its first year, the LPGA had just six members who competed for $15,000 in prize money spread over nine tournaments. Despite this modest beginning, the organization quickly transformed the world of women's golf. It grew rapidly, attracting dozens of new members and thousands of new dollars in prize money contributed by corporate sponsors. By 1953, members of the LPGA could enter more than twenty tournaments with prize money totaling $225,000.

Many of the country's finest golfers joined the group. Patty Berg, Louise Suggs, and Betty Jameson were all, like Babe, former U.S. amateur champions, and all had won the U.S. Women's Open. Suggs had captured the British Women's Amateur championship in 1948, the year after Babe won. Babe had several close rivals, golfers who were capable of beating her on the links on any given day, but she remained the undisputed star of women's professional golf. For several years, she won more tournaments and more prize money than anyone else on the women's pro circuit, and because of her name, she always brought out the biggest crowds.

"Babe changed the game of golf for women—not only by bringing along the LPGA, but by her kind of golf," said Patty Berg. "She came along with that great power game and it led to lower scores and more excitement. . . . And she brought all that humor and showmanship to the game. She humanized it. She was the happiest girl you ever saw, like a kid. Our sport grew because of Babe, because she had so much flair and color. She and I were in competition with each other, but she was a great friend of mine."

Displaying her credentials as a native Texan, Babe twirls a cowboy lasso and steps through the loop. Golfer Betty MacKinnon, a fellow Texan, watches.

No one did more to popularize women's golf. Even so, Babe's uninhibited behavior made some of her competitors shudder. They believed that golf should be a dignified game, and they were offended by her earthy humor and boisterous sense of fun, and by her "five-year-old's hunger for attention," as golfing rival Betty Hicks expressed it.

After a bad shot, Babe was known to shout, "Man! All that work and the baby's dead!" The gallery would howl, her opponents would gasp, and Babe, beaming, would swagger on. When reporters asked her how she was able to hit the ball so far, she replied, "I just loosen my girdle and let it fly!"

"I just loosen my girdle and let it fly!"

Babe demonstrates a difficult "reverse" putt.

"She really was a rather crude person," said Betsy Rawls. "She added a lot of color to the tour when it was needed, but she did not add any dignity to the game."

Babe was fiercely and openly competitive. She would stride into the locker room before a match and call out, "Okay, Babe's here! Now who's gonna finish second?" Above all, she wanted to win, and she would do almost anything to outsmart or unnerve her opponents. She could throw a competitor off her game with a casual "You always hold your putter like that?"

One of Babe's favorite tricks was to fudge on her practice score in order to intimidate the other players. "We were playing in a tournament in Denver and Babe shot an eighty in a practice round," Peggy Kirk Bell recalled. "The press came up and asked her score. 'Oh, about a seventy, I guess,' she said. I was horrified and I said, 'But Babe, you shot an eighty.' She said, 'Well, I could have had a seventy if I tried.'"

During tournament play, Babe almost always seemed calm and cool, no matter how intense the pressure. She rarely displayed her temper. But she could not stand to lose, whether a major tournament or a casual practice game. "She wanted to win," said her close friend and fellow golfer Betty Dodd. "I don't care what she was doing. Cards, pool, Ping-Pong, it didn't make any difference . . . and she was not a good sport about losing either."

Once she was out with three friends, playing for fun, when she missed several putts. "She just stopped," one of them recalled, "stood there and all of a sudden she snapped the putter over her knee like a toothpick. Then she hauled off and threw the pieces into the woods. She scared the rest of us to death. We didn't say a word the rest of the way in."

Babe could be overbearing at times, but for the most part, she won the affection of the women who toured with her. They grinned at her antics, tolerated her boasting, and admired the exuberant energy she brought to every game she played. Patty Berg was one of her biggest fans: "You know people loved the Babe and they clung to her for her wit and her humor and enthusiasm and really for her love of life. She enjoyed winning, playing the harmonica for people, and making them happy. She was a very caring lady."

Babe also enjoyed practical jokes and pranks, a trait carried over from her schooldays. Once on tour, she was rooming with Peggy Kirk Bell at the home of friends in Orlando, Florida. Peggy got up to go to the bathroom. When she returned, Babe appeared to be sound asleep in bed. "But she had stuffed pillows in the bed to make it look that way," Peggy recalled. "She was really under my bed. Just when I was dropping off to sleep, she grabbed my foot. I screeched and leaped a mile and she just laughed and laughed."

Another time, Peggy noticed that her bed kept moving. "I couldn't fig-

Babe plants a kiss on the forehead of her sixteen-year-old caddy, Kent Foley, after winning the Western Women's Open for the fourth time in June 1950.

ure it out. I'd just be off to sleep and I'd feel this jerk. Babe had tied a rope to the springs on my bed and she'd pull it from her bed and jar me. Life was never dull with Babe. She was just a great big overgrown kid who loved living. She loved every minute, more than anyone I've ever known."

Babe had one of her best years in 1950. She captured six major LPGA tournaments, making her the year's leading money winner. And she took a job as the resident teaching pro at the Sky Crest Country Club outside Chicago, the first woman to hold such a post. With her tournament winnings, her salary at Sky Crest, and the fees from her many endorsements, exhibitions, and personal appearances, she had become, as Fred Corcoran, her agent, boasted, "the first woman athlete to bring her annual income up to six figures."

As always, Babe gloried in her stardom. She drove from tournament to tournament in her latest car, a white Cadillac convertible with the name "Babe" spelled out in bright letters on the doors.

Babe and Jim Thorpe, chosen by the Associated Press poll as the top male and female athletes of the first half of the century.

At the end of the year, one of the biggest honors yet came her way. Four times in the past—in 1932, 1945, 1946, and 1947—Babe had been voted Woman Athlete of the Year. In 1950, by an overwhelming margin, the Associated Press poll of sports editors named her both the Woman Athlete of the Year and the outstanding Woman Athlete of the Half Century.

Signing autographs.

☆ ☆ ☆ *Twelve* ☆ ☆ ☆

PARTNERS

*E*ver since their marriage in 1938, Babe and George had been constantly on the go. Traveling back and forth across the country, they had rented or owned homes in Los Angeles, Denver, and most recently Chicago, where Babe was currently teaching. They never managed to stay in any one place long. Despite Babe's restless energy and thirst for glory, she yearned for a permanent home. More than anything, she wanted a place where they could settle down for good.

Finally, she convinced George that they should invest their savings and their future in the purchase of an old Florida golf club, which they fixed up and renamed the Tampa Golf and Country Club. Babe's name alone was enough to attract a large membership. They moved south to live in a converted caddy house right on the grounds. Later they built a large and luxurious home overlooking the golf course.

To all appearances, Babe and George were a devoted and playful couple, fiercely loyal to each other. Babe would not tolerate any criticism of George. And yet their closest friends knew that their marriage was troubled and had been for several years.

Early in the marriage, George had retired from wrestling and taken over the management of Babe's career. He had been a wonderful help to her, a go-getting promoter and shrewd judge of which moves would help build her reputation. He knew more about her golf game than anyone. He'd go out to the golf course with Babe and watch her practice hour after hour, so he could offer suggestions to hone her skills. And he was fre-

George watches Babe practice.

quently at her side during tournaments to offer emotional support. "George and I are a team," said Babe. "I lean a lot on his advice."

"I truly believe she loved him when she married him," Babe's friend Betty Dodd observed. As the years passed, however, the strains on their marriage began to tell. George worked hard to promote Babe's career, but he missed the recognition and attention he had enjoyed during his active wrestling days. His love of the limelight was as great as his wife's. When he felt that Babe was too full of herself, he would corner her and say, "Listen, Babe, I was a celebrity in my right—and don't you ever forget it!"

As Babe's fame grew, she became more independent in her career choices and no longer relied solely on her husband's guidance. When she began to negotiate some of her own deals for personal appearances, without consulting George, he blew up. "George was furious," according to Betty Dodd. "He knew he was losing control of her, that she didn't need him."

Babe and George both said that they wanted children, but that never came to pass. Babe had at least one miscarriage. She told her friend Peggy Kirk Bell, "I'd give up every trophy I ever won if I could have a baby." George said later that they thought of adopting a child, but they were on the road traveling so much of the time, nothing came of that idea.

George was a man of gargantuan appetites, a compulsive eater and heavy drinker who gained weight steadily, ballooning to nearly four hundred pounds. He would peel the wrapper from a stick of butter and eat it like a banana, drip gravy on his shirt in restaurants, and sometimes lift the water pitcher off the restaurant table and drink directly out of it.

He and Babe had heated arguments about his eating habits, his table manners, and his unkempt appearance. A robust, good-looking giant of a man when they first met, he had become, as their friend Betty Jameson put it, "just a big fat slob. I wouldn't want him to come in my house and sit down on the furniture—I don't think I have a heavy enough piece of furniture."

Another source of friction was George's uncontrollable wanderlust, "the itchy foot" as he called it. "He used to say to Babe, 'I'm going to get in the car and just go,' and *bang*, he'd be off," said Betty Dodd. "He might be gone three weeks. Babe never knew."

They fought often, talked about divorce, and spent much of the time apart. Babe's friends felt that she had outgrown George, that he had become a burden to her. And yet Babe and George never separated permanently, and never lost their ironclad loyalty to each other. The tie between them was just too strong. To the press and public, they continued to present themselves as a happily married couple, but those around Babe knew that, despite appearances, she wasn't happy. As time went on, she became increasingly lonely.

Babe met Betty Dodd for the first time at a golf tournament in Miami, Florida, in 1950. The two women were introduced by Bertha Bowen, who asked Babe to help Betty improve her golf game. Betty was nineteen years old, a lanky redhead with freckles, intense brown eyes, and a winning smile. Babe was twenty years older and at the peak of her career. They found they had a lot in common.

"I was pretty much in awe of Babe, who was the outstanding paragon of golf," Betty recalled. "When I first saw her, her hair was dyed red, she was wearing a robin's-egg blue suit with eyes that matched, and she was outstanding. She was not good looking, but she was strong and striking. The minute I saw her, I knew that had to be the Babe. We were introduced, and we struck it off right away, becoming friends from that moment."

Betty visited Babe and George at their new home in Tampa, and from then on, the two women were constant companions. They developed an intimate friendship, a close and lasting bond that would sustain Babe for the rest of her life. Betty admired Babe and looked up to her. "I didn't look on her as an idol, but I admired her ability and athleticism," she recalled. And while Babe rarely spoke about her personal feelings, she apparently saw in Betty the spirited, untamed tomboy that she had been in her own youth. "We had such wonderful times," Betty said. "I would have walked underground to China for Babe in those days. She was the most famous person in the world and I was her protégé."

Babe and Betty became partners in everything they did. The two women traveled almost everywhere together and often played together in tournaments. Betty was a talented guitar player and singer, Babe still had her harmonica, and on tour they would entertain their fellow golfers with impromptu jam sessions.

Babe drives a long one as Betty Dodd (left) and Patty Berg look on.

"They did have such fun together," said Bertha Bowen. "They spoke the same golf language and they enjoyed the same things. They were downright professional with the mouth organ and the guitar. 'Begin the Beguine' was a miracle to hear." Babe and Betty were good enough to make a recording for Mercury and to appear as a musical duo on several network television shows.

Eventually Betty moved in with the Zahariases and lived with them in their Tampa home. At times, sparks flew between her and George. While George resented the close attachment between his wife and the young golfer, he came to accept the arrangement. He and Babe continued to feud, but they were both unwilling to break up their marriage. More often than

Betty and Babe stage an impromptu jam session.

not, Betty was the one who smoothed things over and made peace between them.

Betty recognized that Babe had conflicting feelings of both affection and hostility for her husband. And she understood that Babe wanted to be known as a happily married woman. "She was very loyal to George," said Betty. "She didn't want the world to know that she had those kinds of feelings [of hostility] about George because it had always been the other way."

Babe's career, meanwhile, continued to soar. In 1951, she again dominated women's professional golf, winning seven major tournaments and ending the year as the leading money winner. *Newsweek* magazine called her "Mrs. Golf." *Time* magazine, guessing at her annual income from tournament winnings, exhibitions, and endorsements, labeled her "Big Business Babe."

Mrs. Golf: Babe putts on the eighteenth green.

The year 1952 started out with more tournament victories and with a heavy schedule of exhibition matches. That spring Babe played a cameo role in *Pat and Mike*, a Hollywood movie starring Katharine Hepburn as a championship golfer and Spencer Tracy as Hepburn's manager and love interest. The original script called for Hepburn to beat Babe in their filmed golf match. But Babe refused to lose—even in the movies—and the script had to be rewritten, allowing her to defeat Hepburn by one stroke on the eighteenth green.

Shortly after making the film, Babe entered the hospital in Beaumont to undergo surgery for a strangulated hernia in her left thigh, a painful condition that had been bothering her for some time. She recovered quickly, recuperated at home in Tampa, and was back on the golf circuit by the end of summer. In October she won the Texas Women's Open in Fort Worth for the fifth time. She was on top of the world again. "I felt wonderful," she recalled. But her euphoria didn't last. When the tournament season ended in November, she was exhausted. She went home to Tampa, plagued by persistent fatigue.

"I wasn't feeling wonderful anymore," she wrote. "I wasn't in pain, the way I had been before my hernia operation. . . . Mostly the thing was that I seemed to be tired all the time. When I played a round of golf, I never felt like I wanted to play another nine holes."

Babe felt certain that with a few weeks of rest, she would snap out of it. But when the tournament circuit started up again in 1953, she still felt lethargic and her game was off. A good round would be followed by a disappointing one. She won just one tournament that spring, placed sixth in

Babe grins after winning the first Babe Zaharias Open in Beaumont, Texas, April 1953. Two weeks later, she was operated on for cancer.

another, and was a runner-up several times. At the Peach Blossom–Betsy Rawls Tournament in South Carolina, she had barely enough energy to finish eighteen holes, completely out of the running.

Betty and George both urged her to go back to her doctor for a check-up. But first, she was determined to make a strong showing in the tournament created in her honor by her hometown, the Babe Zaharias Open in Beaumont.

"I'll never know where I got the energy to play that tournament," she wrote. She wanted to win so badly that she somehow found the strength she needed and nosed out her old rival Louise Suggs, winning the Babe Zaharias Open by one stroke on the eighteenth hole.

"That hometown gallery went wild," she recalled. "Betty Dodd and Patty Berg and some of the other girls rushed onto the green and lifted me up in the air. They practically carried me off to the clubhouse. Television cameras were going and everything."

But she was too tired to celebrate. As soon as she could get away, she went up to her room in the clubhouse, collapsed on the bed in her golf clothes, and fell asleep. The next morning, she kept her appointment with her family doctor, W. E. Tatum, who had treated Babe for her hernia the year before.

As Dr. Tatum examined her, Babe recalled, "I could see his face out of the corner of my eye. All of a sudden he just turned white. He didn't say a word. I guess I'd suspected all along what my trouble was. I said to him, 'I've got cancer, haven't I?'"

Recovering from surgery, Babe strolls through the hospital in Beaumont with Betty Dodd.

☆ ☆ ☆ *Thirteen* ☆ ☆ ☆

"I'M NOT A QUITTER"

"*I* remember when Babe came back from the doctor's office after they took the tests," Bertha Bowen recalled. "She was ghastly white. Her lips were just a thin line—as if she had no lips at all. She walked into her bedroom and threw her big brown bag on the chair in the corner and said, 'B.B., I've got it. The worst kind. In all honesty, I'm not worried about myself, but I'm worried about George.' And she meant it, because she knew that he didn't have the stamina that she had to meet reverses like that."

Babe had suspected for some time that she might have cancer, the disease that had taken her father's life. She had noticed symptoms that worried her, but she had confided in only one person, her friend Betty Dodd. "I'd never even hinted at such a thing to George," she wrote. "I continued to keep my cancer fears a secret from him."

Now there was no secret, and the diagnosis came as a shock to everyone. Babe had colon cancer. Her doctors had found a malignancy in her lower intestine. She would have to have a radical operation called a colostomy—a term that Babe had never heard before and that she could neither pronounce nor spell at the time.

To remove the tumor, surgeons would have to cut off part of her lower intestine and reroute the shortened intestinal tract, so that her solid waste could pass through an opening they would create on the left side of her stomach. The operation "changes your anatomy so much you wonder whether you'll ever be able to live your normal life again," Babe wrote. "That was all I could think about when I first got the bad news."

George had broken down in the doctor's office. Weeping bitterly, he kept insisting that Babe did *not* have cancer. Betty was visiting her parents in San Antonio at the time. Babe phoned her and, in a trembling voice, asked her to come to Beaumont, where the operation would take place. "Betty," she said, "I've got cancer. . . . I've got to be operated on. I've got to have a col . . . col . . ."

"She couldn't say the word," Betty recalled. "I said, 'Colostomy?' and she said that's right. It took ten days to build her up for the operation. I moved into the hospital room with her."

Aside from her hernia operation the year before, Babe had never been seriously ill. Her superb physical condition had always been a source of pride and confidence, but now, she felt, her body had betrayed her. She had to face the possibility that her sports career was finished. Her doctor told reporters, "I don't know yet if surgery will cure her, but I will say that she never again will play golf of championship caliber."

The operation on April 17, 1953, took more than four hours. Afterward, Dr. Robert Moore, the chief surgeon, called George and Betty into his office. The colostomy had gone well, he told them, but during surgery, the doctors had discovered that Babe's cancer had spread into her lymph nodes, where it was inoperable. This meant that she could expect more trouble within a year or so. "She's got three strikes against her," Dr. Moore said. He felt that this discouraging news should be kept from Babe—a common practice among cancer patients in the 1950s. George and Betty followed his advice.

Betty stayed in the hospital room with Babe during her recovery, sleeping on a cot. She had put Babe's golf clubs in a corner of the room, where Babe could see them when she woke up every morning. Thousands

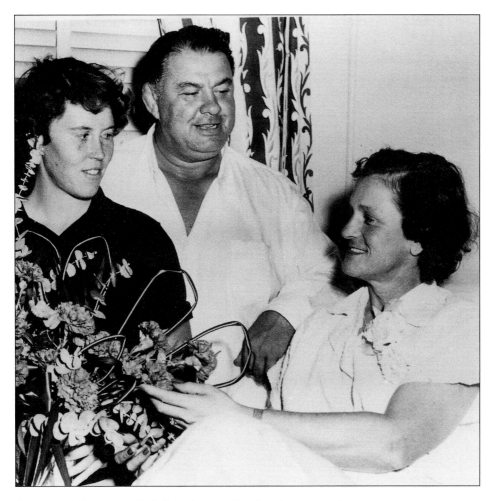

Betty and George at Babe's bedside following her operation.

of get-well letters and telegrams poured into the hospital. They came from all over the world, from people she had never met, some addressed simply "To Babe," with not even a city or state on the envelope. Babe had asked that instead of flowers, well-wishers should send contributions to the Damon Runyon Cancer Fund.

She regained her strength quickly. While she was still recuperating in bed, she began exercises designed to strengthen her leg and arm muscles. And as soon as she got out of bed, she began swinging her golf clubs. Ten days after surgery, she was wandering about the hospital, visiting the children's ward, playing her harmonica, and cheering up everyone she saw.

And while sportswriters had speculated that she would never play championship golf again, she was determined to prove them wrong. She viewed her cancer as a temporary setback, and her recovery as a contest she intended to win.

"All my life I've been competing—and competing to win," she wrote in her autobiography. "I came to realize that in its way, this cancer was the toughest competition I'd faced yet. I made up my mind that I was going to lick it all the way. . . . I was determined to come back and win golf championships just the same as before."

Babe left the hospital on May 18, a month after her operation. She traveled with Betty to her brother Louis's home in Newton, Texas, then visited Betty's parents in San Antonio, and finally returned to Tampa in June, ready to play golf again. "I am feeling wonderful and the col . . . y is working okay," she wrote to Bertha Bowen.

On July 31, just fourteen weeks after her surgery, Babe entered the All-American tournament at the Tam O'Shanter Country Club outside Chicago. "This was so remarkable I still can't believe she did it," Betty recalled. "We were down in Tampa and Babe said to me, 'Let's go play the Tam.' . . . She was determined."

Worried that her artificial intestinal tract might misfunction, Babe asked to be paired with Betty throughout the tournament. "She was familiar with my condition, and could step in and help if I had any trouble," Babe wrote. So Betty played alongside her. George was there too, chomping on his cigar, carrying a sit stick for Babe to rest on between shots, and massaging her shoulders as she sat.

A big crowd had shown up to watch Babe's return to tournament golf, and she was unusually tense. Afraid that she might injure herself, she played cautiously. "I could still bang out some long ones," she wrote, "but I didn't seem to have the control and the touch that you need, especially on the short game."

During the third round of the tournament, "Neither of us was playing well," Betty recalled. "Babe was missing shots and fighting like mad." Finally, Babe became so discouraged that she walked off the green and sat on a nearby bench. "She just sat down and put her head in her hands and sobbed and sobbed. It was the first and last time I ever saw Babe break

Back in action.

(RIGHT)

*Babe gets a kiss
and a hug from
her husband after
playing in the
All-American
Tournament at the
Tam O'Shanter
Country Club.*

down on the golf course. I told her, 'Babe, quit. No one will care. They'll understand.' She looked up at me with tears streaming down her face and said, 'No, no. I don't want to quit. I'm not a quitter.' She pulled herself together. Then she hit a fine drive."

Babe finished the tournament in fifteenth place. Two days later, she entered the World Golf Championship on the same course and took third place. She went on to play the rest of the season, finished sixth among the year's money winners, and won the Ben Hogan Comeback of the Year Award.

She started the 1954 season poorly, tying for fourteenth place in the Sea Island Open, placing seventh in the Tampa Women's Open, then losing a sudden-death playoff to Beverly Hanson in the St. Petersburg Open. She began to have doubts about her comeback. Ten months after her operation, she still tired easily. "People were beginning to ask each other whether I'd ever be capable of winning tournaments again," she wrote. "And I was asking myself the same thing."

Then she hit her stride. She captured the Serbin Women's Open in February and went on to win four more major tournaments in 1954, including the U.S. Women's Open at the Salem Country Club in Peabody, Massachusetts, the biggest title in women's golf. Her spectacular win at Peabody entered the record books as a performance of legendary proportions. A gallery of several thousand spectators watched her shoot 72, 71, 73, and 75 in the four rounds of the tournament, finishing an amazing twelve strokes ahead of her nearest rival, Betty Hicks.

Babe had captured the Women's Open twice before, in 1948 and 1950, but this victory was especially sweet. Immediately after the match, she phoned her surgeon, Dr. Robert Moore, from the golf course to thank him for all he had done. "You did it yourself, Babe," he replied. "It was your faith, Babe . . . that and your courage."

Babe Didrikson Zaharias was voted the outstanding Woman Athlete of 1954 by the Associated Press, the sixth time she had won the award. She was, and remains, the only person to receive that honor so many times. However, no award meant as much to her as her triumphant return to the professional links. A cancer victim with a reconstructed anatomy, she had come back a winner following an operation that left many colostomy patients as semi-invalids. Medical experts and sportswriters had predicted the end of her career. *Never again*, they had said. Babe had proved them wrong.

She was invited to the White House that year to meet President Dwight D. Eisenhower and help launch the American Cancer Society's annual fundraising drive. The president was a dedicated golfer himself. When they were introduced, he shook her hand warmly and said, "How do you do, Mrs. Zaharias." Then he lowered his head and pretended to whisper, "I'll see you later, Babe. I want to talk to you about this game of golf." They did talk golf after a photo session and a ceremony in which Babe received the Cancer Society's symbolic Sword of Hope.

President and Mrs. Dwight D. Eisenhower greet Babe at the White House.

All eyes are on the ball as Babe shoots from the rough.

She started the 1955 season in good form, winning the Tampa Women's Open and the Serbin Diamond Golf Ball Tournament. But then her energy began to flag again. The doctor suggested a vacation. That spring, during a fishing trip with Betty and Betty's sister Peggy on Padre Island on the Gulf of Mexico, Babe woke up one morning with a terrific back pain that grew steadily worse. "Now that I look back," Betty remembered, "this was the beginning of the end. The cancer had returned, but it took *months* to find it."

At first the pain came and went. Babe continued to play golf and to lend her active support to countless cancer fundraising efforts. In an era when cancer was often spoken of in whispers, she was one of the first celebrities with the courage to publicize her condition. By doing so, she became an example of hope to millions of others. "Every time I get out and play well in a golf tournament, it seems to buck up people with the same trouble I had," she wrote.

She went out to Seattle to open a Babe Didrikson Zaharias chapter of the American Cancer Society. Later, Babe and George announced the formation of the Babe Didrikson Zaharias Cancer Fund. And she made many personal appearances and radio and television spots for cancer-fund drives. Whenever she played in a tournament, she would visit cancer patients in the area "and try to raise their spirits." Often Babe and Betty would tour hospital cancer wards together, playing the harmonica and guitar and chatting with the patients, offering words of encouragement from Babe's own experience. In these visits, Babe served as a model to others and forgot, for the moment, her own uncertain future.

After the game: Betty, Babe, and George enjoy a happy moment.

After her fishing trip to Padre Island, she entered three more tournaments, winning one of them, although her game was slowed now and she was often in pain. Finally, after many tests, x-rays, and exams, the doctors found what Babe had feared for a long time—a new cancer in her lower spine. "A radiologist spotted it," said Betty. "In some ways, I wonder if the doctors had kept missing it because they just didn't want to see it. Anyway, it was now just a matter of making her comfortable. There was no way to operate on it."

George held a press conference at the hospital and told reporters that Babe "took the bad news like the mighty champion she has always been. . . . She's not giving up. . . . She never flinched when told she had another cancer."

That summer, back home in Tampa, Babe began to work on her autobiography with the help of a tape recorder and a professional writer. There were times when she felt strong enough to get out on the golf course again, though her drives were weak and she tired easily. Then the pain would return like a missile in the night, sending her back to bed in agony.

In October, Babe's good friend and golfing rival Peggy Kirk Bell came to Tampa for a visit. "She was in great pain," Peggy recalled, "but she knew how much I loved to play golf. That gal got out of bed and insisted that we play. She couldn't get her golf shoes on, they hurt too much. So she played in loafers."

That was Babe's last round of golf. From then on, she was in and out of the hospital, with Betty constantly at her side. "I had such admiration for this fabulous person," Betty said later. "I never wanted to be away from her even when she was dying of cancer. I loved her. I would have done anything for her."

In December, Babe left the hospital long enough to spend the Christmas holidays with Bertha and R. L. Bowen. The day after Christmas, she asked to be driven to a nearby golf course. When they arrived, she got out of the car. She had on her pajamas and bathrobe. Bertha helped her walk over to the eighteenth green. Babe stood there uncertainly, then knelt down and rubbed her hand across the surface of the grass. "I just wanted to see a golf course one more time," she said.

She was failing now, but slowly. It took months for the spreading can-

Still fighting: In and out of the hospital during the last year of her life, Babe goes for a ride with her sister Lillie.

cer to destroy her magnificent athlete's physique. By March 1956, "she was in so much pain she was ready to go back to [John Sealy Hospital in] Galveston," said Betty. "That was it. She never left the hospital."

The tournament season was in full swing. Babe urged Betty to keep up her own golf career and get back into competition. "Go, honey, and play," she told Betty. "Lillie will take care of me." Babe asked her sister to come down to Galveston and stay with her. Lillie rented an apartment near the hospital, but she spent most nights in Babe's room.

"Babe, she knew she was gonna die," Lillie recalled. "She was all over that hospital when she could still walk. She'd go visit the kids in their wards and fool with 'em and make 'em laugh with her card tricks and

BABE DIDRIKSON ZAHARIAS

things, then she'd say to me, 'Don't go see 'em, Lillie, the kids with cancer are so pitiful. They are there without eyes and without mouths. Oh, it's not so bad for me, Lillie, my cancer don't show, it's on the inside. But the children, some of them, oh, Lillie, they are such pitiful things.'"

Babe lingered through the summer. From her hospital bed she could see sunlight glistening on the blue waters of the Gulf of Mexico. Lillie held her hand, just as she had held Babe's hand when they had jumped as daredevils from moving freight trains in Beaumont so long before. George held tearful press conferences for reporters who gathered at the hospital as the end neared. At times he broke down in sobs and had to leave the press room.

Betty was off on tour, playing golf. That's the way Babe wanted it. One afternoon after a tournament in Detroit, players and spectators alike remained at the eighteenth green and gathered around Betty as she began to play her guitar and sing. Someone suggested that people might want to throw their loose change onto the green for the Babe Didrikson Zaharias Cancer Fund. About $5,000 was contributed in Babe's honor that afternoon.

Babe died in Galveston on the morning of September 27, 1956. She was forty-five years old. "I guess she never gave up," Bertha Bowen said. "She kept her golf clubs in the room right to the end."

The *New York Times* reported her death on the front page, recounting the story of her life, her accomplishments, and her courageous three-year battle against cancer. "She didn't know the meaning of the word quit, and she refused to define it, right to the end," said the *Times*. "It is not only the annals of sport that her life has enriched. It is the whole story of human beings who somehow have to keep on trying."

"George, I hate to die," she had whispered toward the end. Then she added, "I'm just learning to play golf."

Even on her deathbed, Babe's sense of humor and her passion for sports still shone through. And that's how her friends remembered her.

"Sometimes I find myself leaning back in a chair thinking about Babe," said Patty Berg, "and I have to smile—with Babe there was never a dull moment. Her tremendous enthusiasm for golf and life was contagious— even the galleries felt good when Babe was around."

Author's Note

Working on this book was like visiting a long-lost friend. I first wrote about Babe Didrikson in *Teenagers Who Made History*, my first book, published in 1961. The chapter on Babe focused on her spectacular performance at the 1932 Olympics, when she won two gold medals and was hailed as a teenage superstar. At the time I wrote, the chief sources on her life were the many newspaper and magazine articles that had appeared over the years and her autobiography, *This Life I've Led*, published in 1955, which states that she was born on June 26, 1914.

Babe's story stayed in my mind. A while back, after writing more than forty books, including a number of biographies, I thought it would be a challenging exercise to go back to my first book and see how I might develop and expand some of those biographical essays in the light of recent historical scholarship. The chapter on Babe Didrikson appealed to me for three reasons: because of its inherent drama; because I wanted to write a book-length biography of an exemplary athlete; and because I suspected that after nearly four decades of changing social values, attitudes, and beliefs, a reexamination of Babe's life and career would be instructive.

The first thing I was surprised to learn was that Babe wasn't a teenager at all during the 1932 Olympics, as she claimed and the world believed. Subsequent biographers have determined that she was, in fact, twenty-one years old (see my bibliography), which does not, of course, diminish her achievement.

And I discovered something that I wasn't completely aware of back then: Babe Didrikson Zaharias broke barriers as well as records. She struggled to transcend stereotypes of how a woman should behave and what a woman athlete should be. She turned out to be a far more complex, contradictory, courageous, and endearing character than I imagined when I wrote about her as a beginning author back in 1961.

Russell Freedman, New York City, 1998

Notes

Unless otherwise noted, references are to books cited in the bibliography.

Chapter 1: Breaking Barriers

Babe, "Before I was even into my teens . . ." is from Zaharias, p. 27.

Reporter, "Is there anything . . ." is quoted in the *Beaumont Sunday Enterprise,* May 3, 1970; Cayleff, p. 23; Lipsyte and Levine, p. 119.

Lillie,"Oh, how that girl . . . " is quoted in Johnson and Williamson, p. 10.

Bell, "Girls in sports . . . " is quoted in Cayleff, p. 20.

de Coubertin, "against the laws . . ." is quoted in Cayleff, p. 12.

Brundage, "You know, the ancient Greeks . . ." is from the *New York Times,* December 25, 1932, sec. 3, pp. 1-2; quoted in Cayleff, p. 102.

Scurlock, "Babe was a very brave girl . . ." is quoted in Johnson and Williamson, p. 22.

London newspaper, "We have not seen . . ." is quoted in the *Beaumont Sunday Enterprise,* May 3, 1970; Cayleff, p. 176.

Chapter 2: The Worst Kid on Doucette

Babe, "Babe Ruth was . . ." is from Zaharias, p. 11.

Alford, "All the boys . . ." is quoted in Johnson and Williamson, p. 53.

Babe, "I stopped to watch . . ." is from Zaharias, p. 25.

Family members, "liked the mistake" and "it was just . . ." are quoted in Cayleff, p. 28.

Lillie, "faster 'n' faster . . ." is quoted in Johnson and Williamson, p. 45.

Piland, "One day I heard . . ." is from the *Beaumont Journal,* October 10, 1975; quoted in Cayleff, p. 39.

Ole, Jr., "She was just . . ." is quoted in Cayleff, p. 34.

Lillie, "She was the best . . ." is quoted in Johnson and Williamson, p. 43.

Babe, "I'd go flying . . ." is from Zaharias, p. 29.

Babe, "There were times . . ." is from Zaharias, p. 16.

Babe, "I'd keep a nickel . . ." is from Zaharias, p. 27.

Lillie, "whistlin' around . . ." is quoted in Johnson and Williamson, p. 48.

Babe, "a wonderful family life . . ." is from Zaharias, p. 16.

Babe, "we had a family orchestra . . ." is from Zaharias, p. 16.

Babe, "What a bang . . ." is from Zaharias, p. 8.

Babe, "When the circus . . ." is from Zaharias, p. 13.

Babe, "Poor Momma!" is from Zaharias, p. 26.

Babe, "Momma, don't run . . ." is from Zaharias, p. 22.

Babe, "My parents . . ." is from Zaharias, p. 22.

Chapter 3: A Texas Tomboy

Babe, "As far back . . ." is quoted in Cayleff, p. 39.

Lockhart, "We all liked Babe . . ." is quoted in Cayleff, p. 40.

Blanch, "The boys . . ." is quoted in the *Beaumont Sunday Enterprise,* May 3, 1970.

Gage, "We had intramural games . . ." is quoted in the *Beaumont Sunday Enterprise,* May 3, 1970.

Lytle, "I saw possibly . . ." is quoted in Johnson and Williamson, p. 58.

Babe, "They said I was too small . . ." is from Zaharias, p. 33.

Babe, "He took the time . . ." is from Zaharias, p. 33.

Blanchette, "I took my studies . . ." is quoted in Johnson and Williamson, p. 60.

Alford, "She worked to excel . . ." is quoted in Johnson and Williamson, p. 54.

Scurlock, "There was an academic group . . ." is quoted in Johnson and Williamson, p. 55.

Scurlock, "Babe was bucking . . ." is quoted in Johnson and Williamson, p. 54.

Classmate, "She was just . . ." is quoted in Cayleff, p. 41.

Reynolds, "Go ahead . . ." is quoted in Cayleff, p. 41.

Cooking teacher, "fled shrieking . . ." is quoted in Cayleff, p. 45.

Classmate, "rough and tumble type . . ." is quoted in Cayleff, p. 41

Cayleff, "The same young woman . . ." is from Cayleff, p. 45.

Smith, "I liked her . . ." is from an interview with the author, April 23, 1998.

Blanchette, "We were a terrific team . . ." is quoted in Johnson and Williamson, p. 60.

Newspaper headlines are quoted in Zaharias, p. 34.

Chapter 4: Star of the Golden Cyclones

McCombs, "How would you like . . ." is from Zaharias, p. 35.

Hughes, "The rest of us . . ." is quoted in Johnson and Williamson, p. 63.

Ole, Sr., "You *go!*" is quoted in Johnson and Williamson, p. 63.

Babe, "You never saw . . ." is from Zaharias, p. 3.

Babe, "I'd never seen . . ." is from Zaharias, p. 36.

Babe, "They started hitting me . . ." is from Zaharias, p. 37.

Babe, "She was a good cook . . ." is from Zaharias, p. 39.

Babe, "Dear 'Tiny' . . ." is from Babe's letters to Tiny Scurlock, Mary and John Gray Library, Lamar University, Beaumont, Texas; quoted in Johnson and Williamson, p. 65.

Babe, "Have gotten a lot . . ." is from Babe's letters to Scurlock; quoted in Johnson and Williamson, p. 66.

Babe, "Those hurdles . . ." is from Zaharias, p. 40.

Babe, "I trained . . ." is from Zaharias, p. 41.

Babe, "I'd go out . . ." is from Zaharias, p. 41.

Babe, "Well, I just barely . . ." is from Zaharias, p. 42.

Babe, "Oh! yeah! . . ." is from Babe's letters to Scurlock; quoted in
     Johnson and Williamson, p. 70.

Daley, "A new feminine athletic marvel . . ." is from the *New York Times,*
     July 26, 1931.

Dallas Morning News, "ace of the local Golden Cyclones . . ." is quoted in
     Johnson and Williamson, p. 73.

Babe, "My picture . . ." is from Zaharias, p. 39.

Teammate, "I admit . . ." is quoted in Johnson and Williamson, p. 75.

Babe, "Heck, 'Tiny' . . ." is from Babe's letter to Scurlock; quoted in
     Johnson and Williamson, p. 75.

Babe, "I know I'm not pretty . . ." is quoted in Johnson and Williamson,
     p. 74.

Scurlock, "Babe's family . . ." is quoted in Johnson and Williamson, p. 77.

McCombs, "I've been studying . . ." is quoted in Zaharias, p. 46.

McCombs, "Never before . . ." is quoted in Johnson and Williamson,
     p. 78.

Chapter 5: The One-Woman Team

The *New York Times,* "Miss Mildred Didrikson . . ." is from the *New York
     Times,* July 16, 1932; quoted in Pieroth, p. 37.

Babe, "the hand would just bounce . . ." is from Zaharias, p. 47.

Babe, "You never heard . . ." is from Zaharias, p. 48.

Babe, "For two-and-a-half hours . . ." is from Zaharias, p. 49.

Babe, "I'm going to win . . ." is quoted in Cayleff, p. 65.

Shiley, "It was so hot . . ." is quoted in Pieroth, p. 42.

Babe, "It was one of those days . . ." is from Zaharias, p. 48.

Wood, "Babe! You did it! . . ." is from Zaharias, p. 50.

Kirksey, "the most amazing . . ." is quoted in Zaharias, p. 50.

Babe, "we danced . . ." is from Zaharias, p. 51.

Newspaper, "Gangway! . . ." is from the *New York Times,* August 2, 1931,
     Sec. 10, p. 6; quoted in Cayleff, p. 66.

Associated Press, "Miss Mildred Didrikson . . ." is quoted in Pieroth, p. 44.

Chapter 6: Going for the Gold

Teammate, "We felt like millionaires . . ." is quoted in Johnson and
 Williamson, p. 83.
Babe, "most of the girls . . ." is from Zaharias, p. 52.
Hall, "Babe was very full . . ." is quoted in Johnson and Williamson,
 p. 84.
Shiley, "She had no social graces . . ." is quoted in Johnson and
 Williamson, p. 84.
Shiley, "by no means overconfident" is quoted in Pieroth, p. 47.
Babe, "I came out here . . ." is quoted in Johnson and Williamson, p. 99.
The *New York Times*, "The Babe is no boaster . . ." is quoted in Cayleff,
 p. 66.
Babe, "I got to meet . . ." is from Zaharias, p. 53.
Rice, "the most flawless . . ." is quoted in Cayleff, p. 84.
Babe, "Folks say . . ." is quoted in Johnson and Williamson, p. 100.
Babe, "To tell you the truth . . ." is from Zaharias, p. 53.
Babe, "like a catcher's peg . . ." is from Zaharias, p. 55.
Babe, "Nobody knew it . . ." is from Zaharias, p. 55.
Babe, "Well, I won again!" is quoted in Cayleff, p. 69.
Daley, "eye-lash victory" is from the *New York Times*, August 5, 1932.
Babe, "If it was horse racing . . ." is from Zaharias, p. 55.
Babe, "the payoff . . ." is quoted in Cayleff, p. 69.
Rice, "There was a wild shout . . ." is quoted in Zaharias, p. 56.
Headlines are quoted in Johnson and Williamson, pp. 4-5.
Lillie, "[We] got up there . . ." is quoted in Johnson and Williamson,
 p. 108.
Babe, "I'm tickled . . ." is quoted in Cayleff, p. 75.
Scurlock, "She's the same . . ." is quoted in Johnson and Williamson,
 p. 110.

Chapter 7: Show Business

Rice, "She is an incredible . . ." is quoted in Johnson and Williamson,
 p. 111.

Sportswriter, "She's capable . . ." is quoted in Cayleff, p. 111.

Advertisement, "Speed—unyielding strength . . ." is quoted in Johnson and Williamson, p. 116.

Gallico, "If Babe said . . ." is quoted in Schoor, p. 65.

Babe, "a bunch of hooey" is quoted in Cayleff, p. 100.

Babe, "I positively did not . . ." is quoted in Cayleff, p. 99.

Babe, "I will do everything . . ." is from the *New York Times,* December 14, 1932, p. 28; quoted in Cayleff, p. 101.

Babe, "Not until this last weekend . . ." is from the *New York Times,* December 24, 1932, p. 19; quoted in Cayleff, p. 102.

Babe, "The pressures . . ." is from Zaharias, p. 68.

Babe, "sorry about . . ." is from Zaharias, p. 69.

Babe, "I had never . . ." is from Zaharias, p. 70.

Babe, "I don't want . . ." is quoted in Johnson and Williamson, p. 119.

Babe, "no woman rivals me . . ." is from the *New York Times,* January 5, 1933, p. 25; quoted in Cayleff, p. 105.

Kertes, "She was a warm . . ." is quoted in Johnson and Williamson, p. 138.

Babe, "Most things . . ." is quoted in Cayleff, p. 118.

Kertes, "at 9 in the morning . . ." is quoted in Cayleff, p. 119.

Babe, "Those people . . ." is from Zaharias, p. 79.

Babe, "It was up to me . . ." is from Zaharias, p. 81.

Teammate, "We played . . ." is quoted in Johnson and Williamson, p. 126.

Teammate, "She was very considerate . . ." is quoted in Johnson and Williamson, p. 127.

Babe, "I made a point . . ." is from Zaharias, p. 75.

New York Evening Post, "Famous Woman Athlete . . ." is quoted in Cayleff, p. 107.

Babe, "I was an extra attraction . . ." is from Zaharias, p. 82.

Babe, "Sometimes in those early barnstorming days . . ." is quoted in Cayleff, p. 109.

Babe, "I like pro sports . . ." is quoted in Johnson and Williamson, p. 130.

Scurlock, "This freakish circus travel . . ." is quoted in Johnson and Williamson, p. 128.

Williams, "It would be much better . . ." is quoted in Johnson and
     Williamson, p. 123.
Gallico, "Muscle Moll" is from *Vanity Fair,* October 1932; quoted in
     Cayleff, p. 86.
Gallico, "look beautiful . . ." is from *Readers Digest,* August 1936; quoted
     in Cayleff, p. 86.
Babe, "People are always asking . . ." is quoted in Cayleff, p. 97.
Babe, "My sports career . . ." is quoted in Cayleff, p. 89.

Chapter 8: A New Sport and a New Image

Babe, "a mixed-up time . . ." is from Zaharias, p. 85.
Babe, "I think I'll shoot . . ." is from Zaharias, p. 86.
Babe, "It was like 1932 . . ." is from Zaharias, p. 87.
Babe, "I'd hit balls . . ." is from Zaharias, p. 89.
Chandler, "We really don't need . . ." is quoted in Johnson and
     Williamson, p. 142.
Parker, "Some women cried . . ." is quoted in Zaharias, p. 93.
Newspaper, "Staging a sensational finish . . ." is quoted in Cayleff,
     p. 125.
Babe, "I was ready . . ." is from Zaharias, p. 96.
Friends, "a bad mistake . . ." etc. are quoted in Cayleff, p. 126; Zaharias,
     p. 98.
Bowen, "I was just furious . . ." is quoted in Johnson and Williamson,
     p. 146.
Babe, "As it all turned out . . ." is quoted in Johnson and Williamson,
     p. 147.
Sarazen, "That was a lot . . ." is quoted in Johnson and Williamson, p. 148.
Babe, "And my jaw . . ." is quoted in Cayleff, p. 122.
Babe, "I wasn't . . ." is from Zaharias, p. 99.
Babe, "If I was going . . ." is from Zaharias, p. 101.
Sarazen, "She was very . . ." is quoted in Johnson and Williamson,
     p. 149.
Bowen, "She used her bravado . . ." is quoted in Johnson and
     Williamson, p. 152.

Bowen, "That monkey . . ." is quoted in Johnson and Williamson, p. 152.

Babe, "like a godmother . . ." is from Zaharias, p. 90.

Bowen, "I was criticized . . ." is quoted in Johnson and Williamson, p. 152.

Babe, "Don't ask me . . ." is quoted in Johnson and Williamson, p. 120.

Bowen, "was eager . . ." is quoted in Cayleff, p. 129.

Rawls, "I think . . ." is quoted in Lipsyte and Levine, p. 129.

Babe, "Some writers . . ." is from Zaharias, p. 103.

Gallico, "I hardly knew . . ." is quoted in Johnson and Williamson, p. 153.

McLemore, "Her figure . . ." is quoted in Johnson and Williamson, p. 153.

Chapter 9: Romance

Babe, "I knew . . ." is from Zaharias, p. 104.

Babe, "What an introduction . . ." is from Zaharias, p. 105.

George, "We kept joking . . ." is quoted in Johnson and Williamson, p. 162.

Babe, "I love to dance" is from Zaharias, p. 108.

Babe, "It sort of built up . . ." is from Zaharias, p. 109.

Babe, "husky and black-haired . . ." is from Zaharias, p. 105.

Babe, "must have helped . . ." is from Zaharias, p. 106.

Hannah, "My Babe . . ." is quoted in Johnson and Williamson, p. 162.

Babe, "His mother . . ." is from Zaharias, p. 111.

Babe, "We're very much . . ." is quoted in Cayleff, p. 139.

Scurlock, "We were so excited . . ." is quoted in Johnson and Williamson, p. 163.

Babe, "We could never . . ." is from Zaharias, p. 111.

George, "We had been happy . . ." is quoted in Cayleff, p. 139.

Babe, "It was a very nice affair" is from Zaharias, p. 112.

Australian press, "magnificent specimen . . ." is quoted in Zaharias, p. 116.

Babe, "Here I'd been . . ." is from Zaharias, p. 119.

Babe, "What I really . . ." is from Zaharias, p. 120.

George, "I had a great . . ." is quoted in the *Beaumont Enterprise and Journal,* January 17, 1973; Cayleff, p. 144.

Babe, "I'd much rather . . ." is from Zaharias, p. 120.

George, "I was sweetheart . . ." is quoted in Cayleff, p. 142.

Babe, "I could hardly . . ." is from Zaharias, p. 122.

Babe, "I wanted to see . . ." is from Zaharias, p. 122.

Babe, "Once I knew . . ." is from Zaharias, p. 125.

Sportswriter, "one of the best . . ." is quoted in Cayleff, p. 146.

Hope, "There's only one thing wrong . . ."is quoted in Zaharias, p. 129.

George, "Your momma . . ." is from Zaharias, p. 136.

Esther Nancy, "You go ahead . . ." is from Zaharias, p. 137.

Babe, "A lot of times . . ." is from Zaharias, p. 137.

Bell, "We didn't know . . ." is quoted in Johnson and Williamson, p. 173.

Babe, "I was really inspired . . ." is quoted in Cayleff, p. 151.

Babe, "The rest of us . . ." is from Zaharias, p. 138.

Babe, "I never could . . ." is from Zaharias, p. 138.

Chapter 10: Superman's Sister

Babe, "This was the first . . ." is from Zaharias, p. 139.

Babe, "I want to establish . . ." is quoted in Cayleff, p. 166.

Babe, "that was the last . . ." is from Zaharias, p. 140.

Bell, "She won everything . . ." is quoted in Johnson and Williamson, p. 174.

Babe, "I hit it straight . . ." is quoted in Cayleff, p. 163.

Babe, "I feel like nuts . . ." is quoted in Cayleff, p. 163.

Babe, "I just love . . ." is from Zaharias, p. 100.

Babe, "I was really ready . . ." is from Zaharias, p. 146.

George, "You need something . . ." is from Zaharias, p. 147.

Babe, "There was never . . ." is from Zaharias, p. 149.

Babe, "Whenever anybody . . ." is from Zaharias, p. 152.

Babe, "I wish . . ." is from Zaharias, p. 154.

Babe, "I went there . . ." is from Zaharias, p. 156.

Babe, "one of those things . . ." is from Zaharias, p. 158.

Babe, "I wish . . ." is from Zaharias, p. 162.

Babe, "So I didn't . . ." is from Zaharias, p. 163.

Spectator, "She must be . . ." is quoted in *Time,* June 23, 1947; Cayleff, p. 173.

Babe, "Pretty soon . . ." is from Zaharias, p. 170.

Manchester Guardian, "Surely no woman . . ." is quoted in Johnson and Williamson, p. 181.

George, "Honey, I could hear . . ." is from Zaharias, p. 178.

Chapter 11: "Okay, Babe's Here!"

Babe, "It got to the point . . ." is from Zaharias, p. 180.

Babe, "It nearly killed me . . ." is from Zaharias, p. 180.

Corcoran, "They were great . . ." is quoted in Johnson and Williamson, p. 183.

Corcoran, "Her barnstorming days . . ." is quoted in Cayleff, p. 180.

Babe, "I honestly . . ." is from Zaharias, p. 183.

Babe, "The fees . . ." is from Zaharias, p. 182.

Corcoran, "Well, okay . . ." is quoted in Johnson and Williamson, p. 185.

Berg, "Babe changed the game . . ." is quoted in Johnson and Williamson, p. 190.

Babe, "Man! All that work . . ." is quoted in Lipsyte and Levine, p. 130; Cayleff, p. 190.

Babe, "I just loosen . . ." is quoted in Lipsyte and Levine, p. 128; Cayleff, p. 176.

Rawls, "She really was . . ." is quoted in Johnson and Williamson, p. 189.

Babe, "Okay, Babe's here! . . ." is quoted in Lipsyte and Levine, p. 122; Johnson and Williamson, p. 192.

Babe, "You always hold . . ." is quoted in Lipsyte and Levine, p. 122.

Bell, "We were playing . . ." is quoted in Johnson and Williamson, p. 192.

Dodd, "She wanted to win . . ." is quoted in Cayleff, p. 194.

Friend, "She just stopped . . ." is quoted in Johnson and Williamson, p. 193.

Berg, "You know people . . ." is quoted in Cayleff, p. 184.

Bell, "But she had stuffed . . ." is quoted in Johnson and Williamson, p. 185.

Corcoran, "the first woman . . ." is quoted in Cayleff, p. 193.

Chapter 12: Partners

Babe, "George and I . . ." is from Zaharias, p. 131.

Dodd, "I truly believe . . ." is quoted in Kahn, p. 72.

George, "Listen, Babe . . ." is quoted in Johnson and Williamson, p. 165.

Dodd, "George was furious . . ." is quoted in Cayleff, p. 201.

Babe, "I'd give up . . ." is quoted in Cayleff, p. 215.

Jameson, "just a big . . ." is quoted in Cayleff, p. 199.

Dodd, "He used to say . . ." is quoted in Johnson and Williamson, p. 164.

Dodd, "I was pretty much . . ." is quoted in Kahn, p. 71.

Dodd, "I didn't look . . ." is quoted in Kahn, p. 72.

Dodd, "We had such . . ." is quoted in Johnson and Williamson, p. 19.

Bowen, "They did have such fun . . ." is quoted in Johnson and Williamson, p. 202.

Dodd, "She was very . . ." is quoted in Cayleff, p. 201.

Newsweek, "Mrs. Golf" is from *Newsweek*, May 14, 1951; quoted in Cayleff, p. 193.

Time, "Big Business Babe" is from *Time*, June 11, 1951; quoted in Cayleff, p. 193.

Babe, "I felt wonderful . . ." is from Zaharias, p. 193.

Babe, "I wasn't feeling wonderful . . ." is from Zaharias, p. 193.

Babe, "I'll never know . . ." is from Zaharias, p. 195.

Babe, "That hometown gallery . . ." is from Zaharias, p. 196.

Babe, "I could see . . ." is from Zaharias, p. 197.

Chapter 13: "I'm Not a Quitter"

Bowen, "I remember . . ." is quoted in Johnson and Williamson, p. 203; Cayleff, p. 220.

Babe, "I'd never . . ." is from Zaharias, p. 199.

Babe, "changes your anatomy . . ." is from Zaharias, p. 5.

Babe, "Betty, I've got cancer . . ." is quoted in Johnson and Williamson, p. 206.

Dodd, "She couldn't say . . ." is quoted in Johnson and Williamson, p. 206.

Doctor, "I don't know . . ." is quoted in Johnson and Williamson, p. 204.

Moore, "She's got three strikes . . ." is quoted in Cayleff, p. 219.

Babe, "All my life . . ." is from Zaharias, p. 5.

Babe, "I am feeling wonderful . . ." is quoted in Johnson and Williamson, p. 208.

Dodd, "This was so remarkable . . ." is quoted in Johnson and Williamson, p. 208.

Babe, "She was familiar . . ." is from Zaharias, p. 217.

Babe, "I could still . . ." is from Zaharias, p. 217.

Dodd, "Neither of us . . ." is quoted in Johnson and Williamson, p. 209.

Babe, "People were beginning . . ." is from Zaharias, p. 219.

Moore, "You did it . . ." is quoted in Cayleff, p. 227.

Eisenhower, "How do you do . . ." is quoted in Zaharias, p. 221.

Dodd, "Now that I look . . ." is quoted in Johnson and Williamson, p. 211.

Babe, "Every time . . ." is from Zaharias, p. 228.

Dodd, "A radiologist . . ." is quoted in Johnson and Williamson, p. 213.

George, "took the bad news . . ." is quoted in Cayleff, p. 233.

Bell, "She was in great pain . . ." is quoted in Johnson and Williamson, p. 214.

Dodd, "I had such admiration . . ." is quoted in Cayleff, p. 203.

Babe, "I just wanted to see . . ." is quoted in USGA video, *Golf's Greatest Women.*

Dodd, "she was in . . ." is quoted in Johnson and Williamson, p. 216.

Babe, "Go, honey . . ." is quoted in Johnson and Williamson, p. 218.

Lillie, "Babe, she knew . . ." is quoted in Johnson and Williamson, p. 217.

Bowen, "I guess . . ." is quoted in Johnson and Williamson, p. 218.

New York Times, "She didn't know . . ." is from the *New York Times,* September 28, 1956.

Babe, "George, I hate to die . . ." is quoted in Lipsyte and Levine, p. 135.

Berg, "Sometimes I find myself . . ." is quoted in Johnson and Williamson, p. 191.

☆ ☆ ☆ ☆ ☆

In Search of the Life Babe Led: A Selective Bibliography

*F*rom early on, Babe Didrikson Zaharias had to fight to prove herself, and if there was anything she loved almost as much as winning, it was boasting about her triumphs. A favorite of the era's sportswriters, always eager to be interviewed, she was willing to say almost anything that could be quoted. She wasn't at all shy about embellishing the facts and promoting a larger-than-life public image.

Babe changed her birthdate so many times, each time shaving off a year or two, that when she died in 1956, the press did not seem to know how old she really was. At the entrance to her burial plot in Beaumont's Forest Park Cemetery, an official Texas historical marker informs the visitor that she was born in 1914, the birthdate claimed by Babe in her autobiography, *This Life I've Led*. Just a few steps away, her marble tombstone gives the year of her birth as 1911.

On her application for the 1932 Olympics, Babe stated that she was born in 1913; she figured, perhaps, that if she could impress the nation's sportswriters as a twenty-one-year-old athletic marvel, she could really wow them as a nineteen-year-old. Approaching early middle age, she muddied the waters a bit more, exercising what was then considered a woman's prerogative, claiming that she was born in 1915, and later, on a visa application, declaring that it was 1919. According to members of her family and to her baptismal certificate (her birth certificate is missing), she was born on June 26, 1911.

Babe's legendary string of golf victories in 1946 and 1947 is another topic of some confusion. The exact length of that winning streak depends on who is keeping count. Babe claimed seventeen consecutive victories, a claim supported by press accounts at the time and memorialized in the record books. However, some golf historians now believe that those records may be inaccurate, and that Babe's streak was broken by a single buried loss after thirteen consecutive wins. Biographers Johnson and Williamson give her credit for seventeen wins, while biographer Cayleff suggests that the string was broken at thirteen.

It isn't surprising, then, that no two sources agree on every single detail of Babe's life as she lived it, and as she said she lived it. Even so, thanks to extensive press coverage during her eventful career, and to interviews conducted while most of the people who knew her well were still alive, the overall picture of her extraordinary personality emerges clearly.

An extensive collection of photographs, newspaper and magazine articles, and personal letters chronicling Babe's life and career is available to researchers at the John and Mary Gray Library, Special Collections, Lamar University, Beaumont, Texas. Babe's press-clipping scrapbooks along with additional photos are on file at the offices of the Babe Didrikson Zaharias Foundation, 595 Orleans, Beaumont. And Babe's high-school yearbooks can be found at the Tyrrell Historical Library, 695 Pearl, Beaumont.

Books About Babe Didrikson Zaharias

Babe has been the subject of two authoritative biographies, both of which are critical sources for this book and indispensable to any student of Babe's life. The first to be published was *"Whatta-Gal": The Babe Didrikson Story*, by

William Oscar Johnson and Nancy P. Williamson (Boston: Little, Brown, 1977), written by a husband-wife journalist team known for their feature articles in *Sports Illustrated*. They based their undocumented but reliable account on extensive interviews with members of Babe's family and with her teammates, associates, and friends, including Lillie Didriksen (Mrs. O. B. Grimes), George Zaharias, Ruth Scurlock, Bertha and R. L. Bowen, Patty Berg, Peggy Kirk Bell, Betty Dodd, and others who convey a vivid sense of Babe's personality but remain protective of her personal life.

Babe: The Life and Legend of Babe Didrikson Zaharias, by Susan E. Cayleff (Chicago: University of Illinois Press, 1995) presents a probing account from the point of view of a feminist historian. Cayleff, a professor in the Department of Women's Studies at San Diego State University, examines the social pressures that Babe confronted in her professional and personal lives, the myths she created about herself, and rumors that she was a lesbian. Cayleff interviewed some of the same people seen twenty years earlier by Johnson and Williamson, along with others who had not been interviewed previously. While Betty Dodd had been interviewed a number of times before, Cayleff's book offers a frank, for-the-record discussion of Dodd's relationship with Babe in a conversation conducted before Dodd's death in 1993.

Other biographies include *Babe Didrikson: The World's Greatest Woman Athlete,* an informed but slightly fictionalized account by Gene Schoor (Garden City, New York: Doubleday, 1978); *Babe Didrikson Zaharias* by Elizabeth A. Lynn (New York: Chelsea House, 1989), a concise and readable account for young people; and *The Incredible Babe: Her Ultimate Story*, by Thad S. Johnson with Louis Didrikson, a compilation of biographical sketches, interviews, press clippings, tributes, sports statistics, and more, privately printed in 1996 and distributed by the Babe Didrikson Zaharias Foundation, Inc., Beaumont, Texas.

Babe's Autobiography

This Life I've Led: My Autobiography, by Babe Didrikson Zaharias as told to Harry Paxton (New York: A. S. Barnes, 1955), was a collaboration with an admiring sportswriter who tape-recorded Babe's reminiscences after her first bout with cancer and a year or so before she died. Babe was not a particularly introspective person; she was, to the end, guarded about her personal life and protective of her public image. There is no attempt at self-analysis here. Even so, the flavor of her personality—her warmth, humor, and irrepressible enthusiasm—comes across with considerable force in this spirited first-person memoir.

Books on Sports and Women in Sports

An informative account of Babe's participation in the 1932 Olympics can be found in *Their Day in the Sun: Women of the 1932 Olympics,* by Doris H. Pieroth (Seattle: University of Washington Press, 1996), which includes a brief history of the games and portraits of other women athletes. *Coming On Strong: Gender and Sexuality in Twentieth-Century Women's Sport,* by Susan K. Cahn (New York: The Free Press, 1994), is a groundbreaking study of female athleticism in the United States that helps put Babe's achievement in a larger perspective. *Winning Ways: A Photohistory of American Women in Sports,* by Sue Macy (New York: Henry Holt, 1996), a book for young people, includes profiles of women athletes from the late nineteenth century to the present and over one hundred photos.

    Idols of the Game: A Sporting History of the American Century, by Robert Lipsyte and Peter Levine (Atlanta: Turner Publishing, 1995), offers lively chapters on Babe and fifteen other outstanding American athletes, ranging from John L. Sullivan to Martina Navratilova. *The LPGA: The Unauthorized Version—The History of the Ladies Professional Golf Association,* by Liz Kahn (Menlo Park, California: Group Fore Productions, 1996), includes biographical sketches and interviews with fifty women golfers, including Babe Zaharias, Betty Dodd, and several of Babe's contemporaries and rivals.

    Among numerous books on golf and golfing, one useful guide is *Inside Sports Golf,* by Roger Matuz (Detroit: Visible Ink Press, 1997). For sports records and statistics in general, my final authority was *The 1998 ESPN Information Please Sports Almanac,* edited by John Hassan (New York: Hyperion ESPN Books, 1997).

A Video

Babe in her dazzling prime can be viewed in *Golf's Greatest Women*, a video narrated by Robert Wagner, Volume 3 of the United States Golf Association's centennial series, *Heroes of the Game*, available from the USGA (phone 908-781-5497).

Babe Didrikson Zaharias Museum

This museum helps Beaumont, Texas, pay tribute to a hometown legend through displays of trophies, medals, golfing equipment, photos, and other memorabilia documenting Babe's life and career. It is located at 1750 Interstate Highway 10 East (exit 854) in Beaumont. Hours are nine A.M. to five P.M. daily. Phone 409-833-4622.

☆ ☆ ☆ ☆ ☆

Acknowledgments and Picture Credits

I am grateful to Raleigh Marcell and Jamie Credle for their hospitality and advice during my visit to Beaumont; to Bea Haley, Babe Didrikson's school friend and teammate, for sharing her memories with me; and to Marjorie Jones, James Cross Giblin, and Evans Chan for their comments and suggests on the manuscript.

For assistance with my research, I'm indebted to the following people, all of Beaumont, Texas: Charlotte A. Holliman, Special Collections, Mary and John Gray Library, Lamar University; Jonathan K. Gerland, Tyrrell Historical Library; Carole Williford and Joe Shamburger, the Babe Didrikson Zaharias Foundation; and Rosemary Cox, the Babe Didrikson Zaharias Museum.

Special thanks to Elizabeth Summerlin, creator and performer of the one-woman stage show, *Hey, Babe!*

The photographs in this book are from the following sources and are used with permission:

AP/Wide World Photos: 12, 43 top, 52, 60, 63, 73, 77, 95 bottom, 103, 106, 109, 114, 116, 118, 121, 123, 125, 126, 130, 133, 134, 135, 137, 138, 145, 146, 147, 155 top and bottom, 157, 158, 159, 161, 164.

Babe Didrikson Zaharias Collection, Special Collections, Mary and John Gray Library, Lamar University, Beaumont, Texas: 17, 19, 21, 22, 24, 29, 31, 28, 39, 42, 44, 50 bottom, 67, 74, 75, 81, 83, 84, 86, 98 left and right, 100, 110, 140, 142, 128, 150, 153.

Babe Didrikson Zaharias Foundation, Beaumont, Texas: 14, 34, 68, 104, 184.

Tyrrell Historical Library, Beaumont, Texas: 27 top and bottom, 30, 32.

UPI/Corbis Bettmann: frontispiece, 8, 10, 40, 43 bottom, 46, 48, 50 top, 54, 56, 58, 61, 64, 66, 70, 79, 80, 88, 90, 91, 93, 95 top, 111, 112, 128, 162.

☆ ☆ ☆ ☆ ☆

Index

Page numbers in **bold** type refer to illustrations.